CONTENTS

LOOKING AT DOCUMENTS

The war that broke out in Europe during the summer of 1914 and lasted until late 1918 was unlike any previous conflict. It was different in scale because a struggle that at first had just five main participants – Britain, France, Russia, Germany and Austria-Hungary – eventually involved soldiers from five continents, making it the first *world* war. It was also different in nature because of the new weapons, vehicles and tactics used, and because civilian populations were affected as never before.

The First World War tells the story of over four years' terrible strife. It explores the political situation that provided the breeding ground for war, as well as its immediate causes. It traces the course of the fighting, from the early 'war of movement', through the grim years of trench warfare, to the final offensives. It looks closely at the wartime experiences of many people, from great military leaders to working women on the home fronts. Finally, it examines briefly the political and social changes that swept the world after the armistice was signed.

To bring this story to life, *The First World War* uses a wide range of documents. They include official treaties, letters written by soldiers, propaganda leaflets, diaries and newspaper reports. You will also find extracts from some of the many novels and poems inspired by the war, both at the time and since. To make the documents easy to read, we have printed them in modern type. Difficult or old-fashioned words or phrases are explained in labels around the text. Photographs of the original documents appear alongside some extracts.

When you are looking at a document, think carefully about its origins. Was it written at the start of the war, when no one realised how bloody the fighting would be, or later, when the conflict had claimed thousands of lives? Who wrote it – a politician who had never been to the front or a soldier who had experienced the horrors of battle? Is it propaganda, more concerned to boost morale than tell the truth? These and similar questions will help you work out how reliable a document is likely to be. But remember that no single document can give you a full picture of an event as complex and momentous as the First World War.

On these pages are a few extracts from the documents used in this book. They have been selected to give you an idea of the variety of documents included, and to explain how and why some were written.

 Many great works of imaginative literature were written by soldiers who participated in the war, and you will find extracts from several of them in this book. This verse comes from a poem by Vance Palmer, an Australian soldier who fought in the terrible Battle of the Somme (see page 35).

I have returned to these;
The farm, and kindly Bush, and the young calves lowing;
But all that my mind sees
Is a quaking bog in a mist – stark, snapped trees,
And the dark Somme flowing.

What does this mean? Some words or phrases are difficult to understand. The captions alongside the documents give explanations of highlighted areas of text. You can find out where the **Somme** was on page 35.

Diaries written by people who lived through the war provide invaluable information about day-to-day activities, either on the fighting fronts or among civilians far from the battle zones. *A French Soldier's War Diary 1914-18* gives an insight into the everyday life of a soldier (see pages 13 and 21).

We are living in the earth, our clothes are thick with dirt, we are itching all over, in our shoes, in our trousers, under our shirts, we can't even nod off for one single moment. Even if the guns are silent, the bugs keep on crawling...

Newspaper reports, interviews and advertisements help to build up a picture of wartime life, as well as highlighting particular events that took place during the war years. In 1915, the German government placed this advertisement (see page 27) in the American newspaper *New York World*. Most passengers who were about to sail on the *Lusitania* took little notice and the ship was sunk with hundreds on board.

The sinking of the *Lusitania*

Travellers intending to embark on the Atlantic voyage are reminded that a state of war exists between Germany and her allies; that the zone of war includes the waters adjacent to the British Isles; that, in accordance with formal notice given by the Imperial German Government, vessels flying the flag of Great Britain, or of any of her allies, are liable to destruction in those waters ...

Government documents from the war years provide an official view of the conflict. In his memoirs, British general Douglas Haig (left) quotes the telegram sent to him by the government after the terrible Battle of Passchendaele in 1917 (see page 45).

The War Cabinet desire to congratulate you and the troops under your command upon the achievements of the British Armies in Flanders in the great battle which has been raging since July 31st...

CHAPTER 1

ORIGINS
EMPIRES AND ALLIANCES

The German ruler, Kaiser Wilhelm II (left), and the British king, George V, were cousins. The family resemblance is clear in this photograph, which dates from 1913.

In the late 19th and early 20th century, the most powerful nations in Europe formed two opposing alliances. Conflict between them grew, ensuring that the conditions for war were present long before troops went into action in 1914.

The German Empire was formed in 1871, following victory in war against France (see page 9). Kaiser Wilhelm II, ruler of Germany from 1888, was determined to turn his empire into a world power, so he built up its industry and its armed forces. In particular, the Kaiser set out to create a navy that would rival Britain's fleet. As a result of this arms race, tension between the two nations grew rapidly.

In 1882, Germany had joined Austria-Hungary and Italy to form the Triple Alliance. These three allies, known as the Central Powers, agreed to help each other in the event of enemy attack. Germany was the alliance's most powerful member. Italy had become a united kingdom in 1861 but was weak and anxious to avoid a war. The Austro-Hungarian Empire was crumbling and its emperor, Franz Josef, struggled to control its 11 nations. Franz Josef also feared Serbia, which aimed to take over some imperial territory (see page 10).

Early 20th-century Britain, ruled by George V from 1910, was a great industrial nation with a worldwide empire. The country's main protector was its mighty navy, so its army was relatively small and military service was not compulsory (as

EUROPEAN ALLIANCES

Triple Entente

Triple Alliance
(Central Powers)

0   300 miles

0   500km

Factories owned by the Krupp family played a major role in Germany's industrialisation programme. They produced steel for shipbuilding, as well as the heavy artillery used to bombard enemy lines during the First World War.

it was in other major European countries). Britain was keen to preserve its own position of power in northern Europe, so eyed Germany's military build-up warily.

After its defeat in the Franco-Prussian War (1870-1), France lost the provinces of Alsace and Lorraine to Germany. This was a great blow to French national pride and the government vowed to win them back. Anti-German feeling in France made the country a natural ally for Britain. So, in 1904, the two nations formed the Entente Cordiale.

The Russian Empire was ruled by Tsar Nicholas II from 1894. Its army was huge but poorly equipped. Russians had no desire for war, but were ready to support the Serbs, their fellow Slavs, against Austria-Hungary. In 1907, the Russians allied with Britain and France to form the Triple Entente. This meant that the Triple Alliance faced potential enemies to east and west. War seemed likely – Germany believed it was inevitable.

BELGIAN NEUTRALITY

In 1839, all the major European powers, including Prussia (later part of the German Empire), signed the Treaty of London. It declared that Belgium should remain permanently neutral in any future conflict. Germany's failure to abide by this agreement played an important role in the eventual outbreak of war (see page 10).

On 28 October 1908, an interview with Kaiser Wilhelm II appeared in the British *Daily Telegraph* newspaper. In it, he assured readers that he had no wish for war. Unfortunately, his forceful language gave the opposite impression.

Here the Kaiser gives his reasons for the growth of the German navy (see pages 26-7).

Assign any bounds means 'put any limits'.

Manifold means 'many different'.

But, you will say, what of the German navy? Surely, that is a menace to England?... My answer is clear. Germany is a young and growing empire. She has a world-wide commerce which is rapidly expanding, and to which the legitimate ambition of patriotic Germans refuses to **assign any bounds**. Germany must have a powerful fleet to protect that commerce and her **manifold** interests in even the most distant seas. She expects those interests to go on growing, and she must be able to champion them manfully in any quarter of the globe. Her horizons stretch far away...

THE ROAD TO WAR

On 28 June 1914, Archduke Franz Ferdinand, heir to the Austro-Hungarian throne, made an official visit to the city of Sarajevo in Bosnia-Herzegovina. His beloved wife Sophie accompanied him. The events that took place on that day finally plunged the world into war.

Bosnia-Herzegovina had been an official part of the Austro-Hungarian Empire since 1908. Its people were Slavs, many of them Serbs. They believed strongly that their nation should be part of the neighbouring Slav state of Serbia. The Serbians shared this view. Some people were prepared to use violence to gain independence from the Austro-Hungarian Empire – including members of a secret society known as the Black Hand.

As Archduke Franz Ferdinand set off through Sarajevo in an open-topped car, seven members of the Black Hand were lying in wait for him. They planned to assassinate the Archduke as part of their campaign for independence. Six of the men failed, but the seventh, 19-year-old Gavrilo Princip, shot and killed both Franz Ferdinand and his wife. Their deaths brought political crisis to Europe.

Austria-Hungary decided to take a firm stand against Serbia, which it believed had supported this act of terrorism. But first Emperor Franz Josef consulted Kaiser Wilhelm II. He wanted to be sure that, if war did break out in the Balkans, Germany would come to Austria-Hungary's aid. The emperor got the assurances he wanted, then took the next step towards conflict. On 23 July, he sent Serbia an ultimatum.

The ultimatum contained many demands. It required Serbia to root out all organisations that were plotting against Austria-Hungary, and to accept the assistance of Austro-Hungarian officials in doing so. When Serbia replied on 25 July, it agreed to most of the demands and rejected none outright. Austria-Hungary, however, had already decided war was necessary. War was declared at 11.10 am on 28 July 1914.

At once, the system of alliances (see pages 8-9) began to operate. Germany had already agreed to back Austria-Hungary, its partner in the Triple Alliance, although Italy remained neutral. Russia sided with the Serbs. France backed Russia, its partner in the Triple Entente. Then, on 3 August, Germany invaded neutral Belgium in order to reach France (see page 12). This prompted Britain to join its French and Russian allies the next day.

When they set off for France in August 1914, German soldiers expected an easy victory and a rapid return home. One of the chalked messages on this train carriage indicates their optimistic mood. It says 'Ausflug nach Paris' – 'Excursion to Paris'.

Like Gavrilo Princip, Borijove Jevtic set out to murder Archduke Franz Ferdinand on 28 June 1914. This extract is taken from his account of that day's events which appeared in the *New York World* newspaper on 29 June 1924.

...we knew what we would do to Francis [Franz] Ferdinand. We would kill him to show Austria there yet lived within its borders defiance of its rule. We would kill him to bring once more to the boiling point the fighting spirit of the revolutionaries and pave the way for revolt... As the car came abreast [Princip] stepped forward from the curb, drew his automatic pistol from his coat and fired two shots. The first struck the wife of the Archduke... in the **abdomen**... The second struck the Archduke close to the heart. He uttered only one word, "Sofia" – a call to his stricken wife. Then his head fell back and he collapsed.

Abdomen is another word for 'stomach'.

An artist's impression of the double assassination in Sarajevo

Herbert Henry Asquith was the British Prime Minister in 1914. He was present in the Houses of Parliament on 4 August when Britain's decision to enter the war was announced. His wife, Margot, recalled what happened next in her autobiography.

The **Speaker** is the official who keeps order in the House of Commons, the elected chamber of the Houses of Parliament.

The declaration was made in the name of King George V.

When the **Speaker** had finished reading the **King's message** all the members poured out of the House, and I went down to the Prime Minister's room... I sat down beside him with a feeling of numbness in my limbs... Henry [the Prime Minister] sat at his writing-table leaning back with a pen in his hand... I got up and leant my head against his: we could not speak for tears. When I arrived in **Downing Street** I went to bed. How did it – how could it have happened?... [later] the clock on the mantelpiece hammered out the hour, and when the last beat of midnight struck it was silent as dawn. We were at War.

10 Downing Street is the London home of the Prime Minister.

Margot Asquith

1914
THE SCHLIEFFEN PLAN

THE GERMAN INVASION OF FRANCE

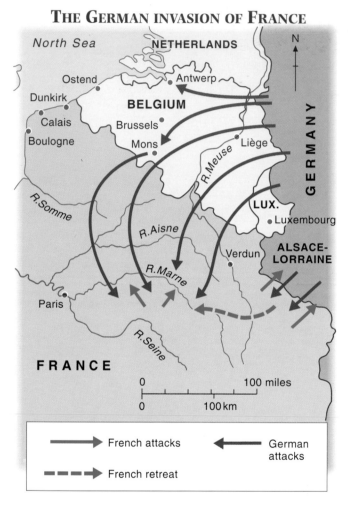

French attacks →
German attacks ←
- - - → French retreat

General Helmut von Moltke

The Germans wanted to win the war quickly and decisively. In order to do so, they believed that it was essential to avoid fighting both France and Russia at the same time. In 1905, Count Alfred von Schlieffen, then Chief of the General Staff, had drawn up a plan to avoid this problem.

The aim of the Schlieffen Plan was to take Paris, defeat the French, and only then deal with the Russian threat in the east. However, in 1914 events did not unfold as the Kaiser and Helmut von Moltke, now Chief of the General Staff, had hoped. The Germans set out for France via Belgium, crossing the border on 4 August. The badly equipped Belgian army resisted unexpectedly vigorously. Nevertheless, the Germans crossed the country in about three weeks. Thousands of refugees fled ahead of them.

The French, led by General Joseph Joffre, were better-prepared than the Germans had believed. Their 'Plan XVII' swung into action as soon as war broke out. Its main aim was to attack the Germans in Alsace and Lorraine (see page 9), then push on to Germany's capital, Berlin. Some troops were also to resist the German invasion of Belgium.

Plan XVII was a failure. French swords and guns were no match for the German heavy artillery in Alsace-Lorraine – over 40,000 Frenchmen died there between 20 and 23 August. The survivors retreated into France, where they joined the armies trying to push back the Germans. But the French were still overcome with ease.

Germany had hoped Britain would stay out of the fighting. But the British Expeditionary Force (BEF), led by Sir John French, set out for Belgium soon after it was invaded. On 23 August, the BEF met a large German army at Mons. Following a day-long battle, the British were forced to retreat south into France.

The French had been pushed back to the River Marne, where the retreating British joined them. The Germans were just 40km from Paris. But instead of heading west and attacking the city as planned, the exhausted German troops turned east to the Marne. Meanwhile, Joffre brought French reinforcements from Paris. At the Battle of the Marne on 5 to 9 September, France and Britain forced Germany back to the River Aisne. In the west, the Schlieffen Plan was in tatters.

A line of Belgian refugees queuing for food hand-outs

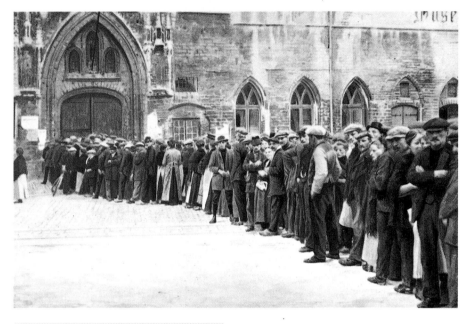

 Henri Desagneaux served in the French army during the First World War. Many years afterwards, in 1971, his diary of the war was published. This extract from *Journal de Guerre 14-18* (*A French Soldier's War Diary 1914-18*) tells of the refugees who made their sorry way across France during the early days of the fighting in 1914.

The **bourgeois** means 'the middle class'.

Requisition officers were military officials responsible for collecting goods and equipment that the armed forces needed in wartime.

Evelyn, Princess Blücher, was a British woman who was married to a German count. She spent 1914-18 in Berlin, and in 1921 published a memoir of those years. Here she describes how hard it was for both the German and the British public to find out what was really happening.

This was untrue propaganda.

Nags is an informal word for 'horses'.

25 August, Tuesday
Refugees arrive from all directions, a mixture of every class of society: the peasant carrying his little bundle; the worker with a few old clothes; small farmers, shopkeepers with their cases, finally the **bourgeois**, dragging along a dog or a trunk... Men, women, children, and old folk are huddled together in any vehicles they could find. What a sad sight it is to see the old carts drawn by **nags** that even the **requisition officers** refused; these poor people, distressed, leaving their homes and their possessions, without knowing whether they will return.

BERLIN, September 18, 1914.– Strange that we hear so little of the fighting round Paris. We have all been expecting to hear of their [the Germans'] triumphant entry every day. The fighting, they say, is very hard, and there are tremendous losses on either side, but I am beginning to think the tide has turned against the Germans, hence this sudden silence... We have at last discovered means of buying the Times [newspaper]... at last we can see what the English are really doing or thinking... What curious reports are being circulated... Berlin is in flames, and in a state of starvation, panic, and revolution. How shall we ever know the truth in any country?

THE EASTERN FRONT

The ill-fated Schlieffen Plan underestimated the Russians, as well as the British and French. The Germans had assumed that the vast Russian army would take at least six weeks to lumber into action in the east. But they were wrong and their miscalculation cost them dear.

Russia had about one-and-a-half million permanent soldiers. On 7 August, about 370,000 of them, in two separate armies, invaded Germany. Meanwhile, three million more Russians were mobilised. The speedy Russian invasion realised the Germans' worst fear – they would have to fight on two fronts, the Eastern and the Western, at the same time. General von Moltke immediately sent more troops

east, weakening his forces in Belgium. He also placed two new commanders at the head of the Eastern Front armies, Paul von Hindenburg and Erich Ludendorff.

The Russian forces easily outnumbered the Germans. However, they were badly trained, led and equipped – there was just one machine-gun for every 1000 men. Many soldiers did not even have their own rifle. The commanders of the two armies, Alexander Samsonov and Pavel Rennenkampf, loathed one another, so did not communicate effectively. Finally, the Russians' radio messages were not coded, so the Germans quickly discovered their battle plan.

The plan was straightforward.

The two Russian armies would separate to make their way around the Masurian Lakes in Germany's northeast corner. Then they would come together again, trapping the hapless German troops between them. However, once the Germans became aware of what was intended one of their leaders, Lieutenant Colonel Max Hoffmann, devised a counter-plan. The German forces would strike while the Russian armies were still apart.

Samsonov's army was the first to arrive west of the lakes. From 26 to 31 August it was crushingly defeated by the Germans at the Battle of Tannenberg. About 80,000 Russians were killed – almost all

THE EASTERN FRONT 1914-16

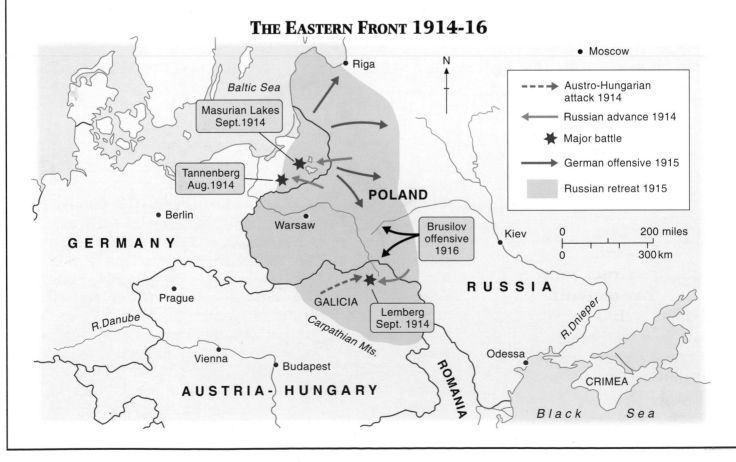

German troops advance into a village during the Battle of Tannenberg. Artillery fire has destroyed several of the buildings along the street.

the rest were taken prisoner. The Germans then headed east to attack Rennenkampf's army at the Masurian Lakes. About 125,000 Russian soldiers met their deaths during the second week of September. The remainder fled back to Russia. These were stunning German victories, but bought at the cost of diverting much-needed troops from the Western Front.

Evelyn, Princess Blücher

AUSTRO-HUNGARIAN ATTACKS

Austro-Hungarian armies were active in 1914, too. On the Eastern Front, they attacked the Russians in Galicia, far south of the German forces. Their early victories were reversed on 8-12 September, when Russian troops led by Alexei Brusilov defeated them overwhelmingly at Lemberg (see map page 14). The Austro-Hungarians invaded Serbia on 12 August. They occupied the capital, Belgrade, on 2 September, but were driven out by mid-December. About 200,000 Austro-Hungarian troops died in the fighting.

Posterity means 'future generations'.

In this second extract from her memoir, Evelyn, Princess Blücher (see page 13) describes the aftermath of Tannenberg, as reported in Germany.

BERLIN, October 14, 1914.—The victory of Tannenberg will go down to posterity as one of the most marvellous of modern times. Some of the horrors of it are so ghastly that an eye-witness, an officer, who has just returned from there, says it will live in his dreams to his dying day. The sight of thousands of Russians driven into two huge lakes or swamps to drown was ghastly, and the shrieks and cries of the dying men and horses he will never forget...

AN ENGLISH WIFE IN BERLIN

A PRIVATE MEMOIR OF EVENTS, POLITICS, AND DAILY LIFE IN GERMANY THROUGHOUT THE WAR AND THE SOCIAL REVOLUTION OF 1918

BY

EVELYN, PRINCESS BLÜCHER

SIXTH IMPRESSION

LONDON
CONSTABLE AND COMPANY LTD.
1921

THE 'RACE FOR THE SEA'

After the Battle of the Marne on the Western Front (see page 12), both Germany and the Allies (Britain and France) wanted to avoid another head-on clash. So they began the so-called 'Race for the Sea'.

This race was in part what its name suggests – a headlong dash northwest towards the English Channel. However, although both sides wanted to take control of the coastal ports, the main aim was to get ahead of the enemy by going around its flank (side). If successful, this would allow troops to wheel back and surround their opponents.

After the German retreat from the Marne, Helmut von Moltke was replaced by Erich von Falkenhayn. This able general oversaw the German push towards the sea, which was the first to begin. At the outset, many German troops were still in Belgium, fighting for the town of Antwerp. When it fell on 10 October, some moved west to join the forces heading for the coast.

French troops under Joffre and the British Expeditionary Force (BEF) under Sir John French quickly followed the Germans. Outflanking proved impossible, but the opposing armies fought several battles. The most important happened at Ypres in Flanders. It began on 12 October and lasted for over a month. The Germans rushed in about 100,000 extra, untrained men to try to seize a victory. But the Allies held the town.

This was no great triumph, however. Sir John French, leader of the BEF, was weak and indecisive. About 50,000 men in the BEF were killed or injured at Ypres. French casualties in the battle were also high – about 250,000 dead and wounded. The terrible losses on all sides were rewarded not by victory but by stalemate.

Ypres marked a turning-point. The early 'war of movement' across large areas of ground ended there. It was replaced by an almost static 'war of attrition', designed to wear the enemy down gradually. This new type of warfare was fought from trenches. The Germans had dug the first trenches by the River Aisne (see page 12). After Ypres, a 644-km line of trenches was built, stretching from the coast almost to Switzerland.

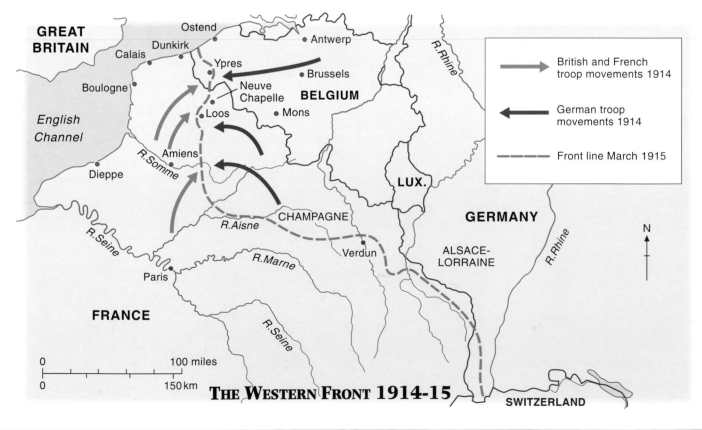

THE WESTERN FRONT 1914-15

TRENCH TRUCES

When the war broke out, German troops were assured that the fighting would be over 'before the leaves fall from the trees'. The Allies expected victory to be theirs by Christmas. But by December, men on both sides were living in trenches. Many had learned to respect their enemies' bravery. On Christmas Eve 1914, German, French and British soldiers sang carols, shouted greetings to their opponents, or even met them in No Man's Land (see page 18). Officers soon put a stop to these truces. By 1915, troops were once again prepared for combat.

British and German soldiers socialising in Belgium on Christmas Day 1914

 Lord Kitchener was the British Secretary of State for War from 1914. He realised that the country's professional army was not large enough, so he recruited hundreds of thousands of volunteers. In this letter, dated 3 December 1914, Captain E. Balfour, a BEF member, explains what he believes this will mean.

...the new Campaign is going to be fought and won by a great half-trained National Army – where you've got to take what you can get and not laugh at people for being a certain class or making fools of themselves. But if the old Army is going to be worth its salt and remain the backbone of the show, it's got without jealousy and in humbleness to allow itself to be absorbed into a less efficient whole ...

The man in the middle of this British army recruitment poster is Lord Kitchener. His stony stare and pointing finger were hard to resist. The flags on the poster are those of the Allies in 1914 (from left to right: Belgium, Russia, the United Kingdom, France and Japan).

Schnapps is a strong alcoholic drink popular in Germany.

 In this extract, a German lieutenant named Johannes Niemann describes the events that took place during a truce at Christmas 1914.

A **dugout** was a shelter cut in a trench wall or floor.

Next morning... my orderly threw himself into my **dugout** to say that both the Scottish and German soldiers had come out of the trenches... I grabbed my binoculars and... saw the incredible sight of our soldiers exchanging cigarettes, **schnapps** and chocolate with the enemy. Later... a real football match got underway.

TRENCH SYSTEMS

Western Front soldiers dug trenches to defend themselves against enemy fire. At first, these trenches were little more than long, muddy holes. However, as the stalemate continued, complex trench systems developed.

Many early trenches were only head-height and had unsupported earth walls. The earth removed to create the trenches was piled up to form defensive banks, called parapets at the front and parados at the back. Gradually, both parapets and parados were reinforced with sandbags and solid floors were built from duckboards. Wood was used to shore up trench sides. Some trenches were dug deeper, and coils of barbed wire were placed in front of them to deter enemy attacks.

Single trenches slowly grew into mazelike trench systems. Their layout varied according to the

nationality of the army and the nature of the battlefield, but they shared many features (see diagram page 19). The trench area closest to the enemy was called the front line. From the foremost trench, the fire trench, men shot at their opponents. Fire trenches were built in a zigzag shape, so that if a shell exploded, its blast could not travel far. A cover trench was often built about 30m behind the fire trench. It held more troops, ready to defend the front line if the enemy broke through.

Seventy or more metres behind the front line were the support trenches, where additional soldiers waited to be called into action. The British and Germans, but not usually the French, also had troops in reserve trenches even further back. German trench systems grew ever more complex. Some eventually extended 22km from the front.

Running roughly at right angles between the defensive trenches were communications trenches. They were often full of troops moving to and from the front, but also provided a link with command posts, first-aid stations and kitchens in the support and reserve trenches. Trench extensions called saps formed part of many trench systems, too. Some led part way to the enemy lines and were used as listening posts. There, soldiers tried to hear enemy activity through the mud walls.

The opposing front lines were separated by an area of open ground between about 70m and 700m wide. This was 'No Man's Land', where soldiers died in their hundreds of thousands.

British troops make their way along a trench in France. The sandbags and wooden wall supports can be seen clearly. The duckboards that form the floor are just visible beneath the men's feet.

OBSERVATION POSTS

Heavy guns, known as artillery, did not fire their shells from the trenches. They were based behind the lines and bombarded the enemy from there. However, artillerymen needed to know the exact positions of their targets to avoid wasting ammunition or even hitting their own lines. So they set up observation posts on the front line and relayed information back to their comrades using field telephones (see page 43).

George Coppard went to war aged just 16. He was an ordinary private soldier who served as a machine-gunner. In 1969, Coppard published *With a machine gun to Cambrai*, an account of his wartime experiences.

Six feet is about 1.8m. One foot equals approximately 30 centimetres.

The trenches at le Touquet were in a very good condition, in parts almost like demonstration models. About **six feet** in depth from the top of the parapet, they were floored with duckboards, and were wide enough for two men to pass comfortably. A **fire-step** a foot or so high ran along each section of trench, enabling troops to adopt a good firing position in case of attack. The few dugouts that there were afforded very little more protection than a **shell-hole**. Most of them were just excavations at the bottom of a trench sufficient to crawl into and stretch out for sleep...

A **fire-step** was a small, raised platform at the front of a trench. By standing on the step, soldiers could see the enemy lines.

A **shell-hole** was a crater produced by a shell. Soldiers trapped in No Man's Land often hid in them.

Conditions in the support and reserve trenches were better than on the front line, especially for officers. In his autobiography *Goodbye to All That* (1929), the famous English poet and novelist Robert Graves tells of an officers' dugout in France.

This diagram shows a typical First World War trench system as seen from above.

At battalion headquarters, a dugout in the reserve line, about a quarter of a mile behind the front companies, the colonel... shook hands with us and offered us the whisky bottle... this dugout happened to be unusually comfortable, with an ornamental lamp, a clean cloth, and polished silver on the table... Pictures pasted on the papered walls; spring-mattressed beds, a gramophone, easy chairs: we found it hard to reconcile these with the accounts we had read of troops standing waist-deep in mud, and gnawing a biscuit while shells burst all around.

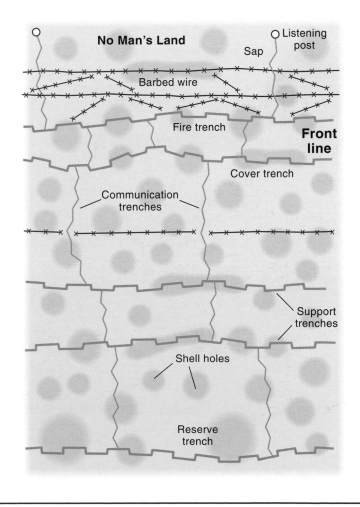

No Man's Land

Listening post

Sap

Barbed wire

Fire trench

Front line

Cover trench

Communication trenches

Support trenches

Shell holes

Reserve trench

LIFE IN THE TRENCHES

The life of troops at the front veered between two extremes – day after day of monotonous routine followed by horrific bouts of fighting. The dreadful living conditions, however, were a constant feature.

In theory, soldiers stayed in the front line for only about a week before a period of respite in the support or reserve trenches. However, replacements sometimes failed to arrive, forcing soldiers to remain at the front for two or even three times longer. After a tour of trench duty, men usually rested at billets behind the lines. There they organised plays, film shows and sports events, and spent their money on drink and women.

Days on the front line followed a routine. Attacks often began at dawn, so soldiers were roused slightly earlier. They then prepared for possible enemy action, while sentries peered out over No Man's Land. After breakfast, men began their duties. Some repaired shell damage. Some collected mail, food and ammunition from support and reserve trenches. Everyone cleaned their weapons and wrote letters home when they could. They also slept to make up for the hours spent working during the night. Sentries always kept a look-out, often using periscopes.

At night, soldiers ventured outside the trenches to carry out more dangerous tasks. Patrols repaired barbed wire defences or gathered information at listening posts. Raiders made their way to enemy lines and launched ferocious surprise attacks. Men without special duties spent the night trying to sleep in damp, cramped dugouts.

Soldiers were always at risk from snipers (see document page 21), but the danger from the enemy was far greater during attacks. Before an attack began, artillery hurled shells into the trenches, causing hideous injuries and deaths. Troops who went 'over the top' – clambered out of the trenches to launch an attack – faced machine-gun fire and more shells. Troops whose trenches were seized faced grenades, rifles, bayonets and knives. Inventions such as gas and tanks steadily added to this array of weapons.

Men developed strategies to cope with their grim lives. They formed close friendships, cracked jokes, sang and sometimes grew very superstitious or religious. Many ordinary soldiers also developed a strong sense of comradeship with their enemy counterparts who were often seen as fellow-sufferers in a war devised by far distant officers and politicians.

A soldier looks through a periscope built into the wall of the trench. Periscopes were life-savers because they allowed look-outs to observe enemy lines without turning themselves into sniper targets.

UNDERGROUND SQUALOR

The everyday squalor of life in the trenches was a constant trial. Insufficient water for washing and unhygienic latrines spread disease. Rain turned the ground into a sea of sticky mud and filthy water, and soldiers who stood in this mixture for too long developed trench foot. Rats infested the trenches. Not only did they steal men's food, they were also carriers of lice, whose bites caused illnesses such as trench fever. Lice clung to hair, skin and clothes, and soldiers spent hours removing them, a process that the British called 'chatting'.

This underground cook-house on the Western Front trenches shows the dirty and unhygienic conditions in which troops were forced to live.

 George Coppard (see page 19) explains how swiftly snipers killed, and tells how a friend became a victim.

British troops called the Germans **Jerries**.

A **telescopic sighted rifle** is fitted with a mini-telescope that gives the user a good view of the target.

Stand to was the order given to British troops before dawn. Men had to take up their positions on the firesteps or in the trenches below.

Lulled by the quietness, someone would be foolish and carelessly linger with his head above the top of a parapet. Then, like a puppet whose strings have suddenly snapped, he crashes to the bottom of the trench... A Jerry sniper with a telescopic sighted rifle... has lain patiently, for hours perhaps, watching our parapet for the slightest movement... A pal of mine named Bill Bailey... died in this way... It was early morning and stand to was over. The fire was going nicely and the bacon was sizzling. I was sitting on the firestep and just as I was about to tuck in Bill crashed to the ground...

George Coppard in 1980

 In this extract, Henri Desagneaux (see page 13) describes how the misery of being dirty and lice-infested added to the horror of battle.

When water was short, it could not be spared for shaving.

We are living in the earth, our clothes are thick with dirt, we are itching all over, in our shoes, in our trousers, under our shirts, we can't even nod off for one single moment. Even if the guns are silent, the bugs keep on crawling. God how filthy we are! Fifteen days' growth of beard, and for the last eighteen days I haven't taken my shoes off or had a change of underwear. We have no water to wash in, just mud all around us.

CHAPTER 3

1915

GALLIPOLI

THE GALLIPOLI CAMPAIGN

The First World War entered a new phase in 1915. More countries joined the conflict, and the fighting spread beyond the Eastern and Western Fronts. The Allies' year began with a doomed attack on Turkey.

By the 20th century, the 600-year-old Ottoman (Turkish) Empire was fading fast. However, the Central Powers welcomed it as an ally in October 1914. In 1915, British politician Winston Churchill suggested an attack on Turkey. He believed that the war would never be won in the trenches of Western Europe, but that Germany could be defeated by crushing its weaker ally. The Russians, whom the Turks had attacked on entering the war, were also calling for an Allied assault on Turkey.

Many politicians and military men opposed Churchill's plans. However, Lord Kitchener (see page 17) decided to go ahead. The aim of the campaign was to take over Constantinople, Turkey's capital. To do so, the British and French navies first set out to capture the Dardanelles – the strait of water that runs into the Sea of Marmara, on whose edge the city stands. Part of the battle plan was to destroy forts on the Gallipoli Peninsula, which forms the Dardanelles' northern coast.

The bombardment of the Peninsula began on 19 February 1915. Although it was partially successful, the Turkish gunners continued to fire, making it difficult for minesweepers to clear the seas of mines. Nevertheless, on 18 March the attacking navies tried to force their way through the Dardanelles. Mines blew up three ships and damaged three more. The officer in charge of the operation, Vice-Admiral John de Robeck, then called for assistance from land forces.

About 75,000 troops were sent to Gallipoli. As well as British and French men, there were many Australians and New Zealanders (Anzacs). None had any battle experience. General Sir Ian Hamilton, who had only limited knowledge of Turkey and its army, was in command. The invasion began on 25 April, with the main landings

General Sir Ian Hamilton (in the front on the far left) puts on a brave face as he leaves Gallipoli. Until 1915, he had been a successful military commander. After Gallipoli, he was never given a senior post again.

This painting shows the landing at Anzac Cove in April 1915. Turkish gunfire is exploding all around the Allied soldiers as they clamber ashore.

at Anzac Cove and Cape Helles. The Turks had strengthened their defences and were able to resist most efforts to advance inland. The result was more fruitless trench warfare.

On 6 August, a second wave of Allied invasions took place at Suvla Bay. They were similarly unsuccessful and the troops suffered dreadfully in the sweltering summer heat. Finally, on 7 December, the decision was taken to evacuate. This process was completed by 9 January 1916. The whole disastrous campaign had cost about 46,000 Allied lives.

THE SALONIKA FRONT

In September 1915, Germany gained another ally. This was Bulgaria, a Balkan neighbour of Serbia. The Bulgarians hoped that if the Central Powers won the war, they would be granted a chunk of Serbian land. In October, British and French troops were sent to Salonika in northern Greece, which bordered Bulgaria and Serbia. They failed to prevent a Bulgarian invasion of Serbia, but thousands of Allied reinforcements were still sent to the region. There they remained for the rest of the war. They were known as the 'forgotten army'.

As members of the British Empire, Australia and New Zealand were soon drawn into the war. British incompetence and the courage of their own Anzac troops made Gallipoli a turning-point. From then on, both countries felt themselves to be truly independent nations. Keith Murdoch, an Australian journalist, expressed his personal views about Gallipoli in a letter to Australian Prime Minister Andrew Fisher. This is an extract from his letter.

Hamilton's poor planning and numerous other failures led to his dismissal in October 1915.

I visited most parts of Anzac [Cove] and Suvla Bay positions, walked many miles through the trenches, conversed with the leaders and what senior and junior officers I could reach, and was favoured in all parts with full and frank confidence... This was always a hopeless scheme, after early May, and no one can understand why Hamilton persisted with it... A strong advance inland from Anzac has never been attempted. It is broken, rough, scrubby country, full of gullies and sharp ridges, and it is all within easy range of the Turkish forts at the Narrows... No serious advance could be made direct inland at this quarter.

THE EUROPEAN FRONTS

The war on the Western Front continued in 1915, but it lacked focus after the failure of the early plans. Co-operation between the French, under General Joseph Joffre, and the British, under Sir John French, was often unwilling and ineffective. On the Eastern Front, the Germans advanced far into Russian-controlled Poland.

On 10 March, the British attacked the German line at Neuve Chapelle, France. The pre-battle bombardment was brief because of an ammunition shortage. As a result, the Germans had little warning and the British were able to take the village. However, a long wait for reinforcements and a collision between advancing troops gave the Germans time to strike back and the battle ended on 12 March. This pattern of early

Two British soldiers wearing primitive gas masks demonstrate how to use a Vermorel sprayer. It contained a chemical that neutralised chlorine, a gas that the Germans began to use as a weapon in 1915.

Sir John French

success followed by collapse was to be repeated many times.

On 22 April, the Germans launched an offensive at Ypres. During the battle, they used gas – chlorine – for the first time. It engulfed French troops, many of them from France's Algerian colony, as well as British and Canadian forces. The results were terrible but effective. However, the battle gave the

Germans no lasting advantage and ended on 25 May.

The French launched a major offensive in the Champagne region on 25 September. They broke through the German front line, but were unable to overcome strong second-line defences and withdrew on 6 October. Further north, the British attacked and took Loos. But they again failed to build on their success because reinforcements were too far away. Sir John French continued the battle long after it was worthwhile, sacrificing thousands of lives. In December he was replaced by General Sir Douglas Haig.

The Germans had been dismayed by the defeat of Austria-Hungary in 1914 by the Russians at Lemberg (see page 15). So they decided to support their ally in a counter-attack on Russian Poland in the east. On 2 May 1915, troops led by General August von Mackesen stormed into Galicia. Later, troops under Paul von Hindenburg advanced further north. By November 1915, the Russians had retreated nearly 500km and lost much of Poland. Russian ruler Tsar Nicholas II and his people were utterly humiliated – but determined to fight back.

THE ITALIAN FRONT

Like the Central Powers, the Allies gained new members in 1915. The most important was Italy. Before the war, it had been a partner of Germany and Austria-Hungary in the Triple

Alliance (see page 8). When war broke out, it remained neutral. Both sides then tried to gain Italy's allegiance by promising it a share of Austro-Hungarian land after the conflict was over. The Allies offered the bigger bribe so, on 23 May 1915, Italy declared war on Austria-Hungary. Fighting on the Italian Front between the two countries was long and hard (see page 45).

Italian troops fighting in the Alps in 1916

This description of the aftermath of the 1915 Battle of Ypres comes from *A Fatalist At War* (1929) by German soldier Rudolf Binding.

Chlorine gas is greenish-yellow.

The effects of the successful gas attack were horrible. I am not pleased with the idea of poisoning men. Of course, the entire world will rage about it first and then imitate us. All the dead lie on their backs, with clenched fists; the whole field is yellow... The battlefield is fearful. One is overcome by a peculiar, sour, heavy, and penetrating smell of corpses. Rising over a plank bridge you find that its middle is supported only by the body of a long-dead horse. Men that were killed last October lie half in swamp and half in the yellow-sprouting beet-fields. The legs of an Englishman, still encased in puttees, stick out into a trench...

The first Battle of Ypres took place in October 1914.

Puttees formed part of the British army uniform. They were cloth strips wound around the lower half of the leg.

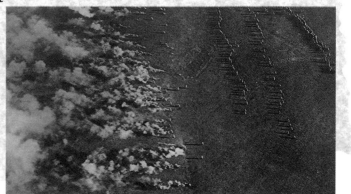

A German gas attack in 1915, photographed from the air

THE WAR AT SEA

Britain had ruled the seas for many years before the First World War began, and the Royal Navy was the nation's pride. Kaiser Wilhelm II's determination to make the German High Seas Fleet equally strong was an important cause of the conflict.

The Kaiser, backed by Admiral Alfred von Tirpitz, started to build up his navy in the late 19th century. Soon afterwards, Admiral Sir John Fisher, Britain's First Sea Lord, began to overhaul the Royal Navy and ordered a warship that would outperform all others. The result was the *Dreadnought*, launched in 1906. The new vessel gave its name to a class of ship and the Germans soon built some of their own. By 1914, they had 13 dreadnoughts, but the British kept their supremacy with 24.

Just before the outbreak of war, the main British fleet moved to Scapa Flow, off the Orkney Islands, to take control of the North Sea. In late 1914, German ships shelled towns on Britain's east coast, including Scarborough. However, the ships were chased away by British battle cruisers. They returned to their own ports and did not venture out again until the Battle of Jutland (see page 27). This was not only because the British were penning them in – the Kaiser did not want to risk the costly dreadnoughts in an all-out battle.

Keeping the German fleet in port was part of a wider naval blockade. The Royal Navy stopped and inspected all ships from neutral countries, confiscating food or raw materials bound for Germany. The Germans began to suffer serious shortages and introduced rationing. In February 1915, they struck back by beginning submarine warfare.

The German submarines, known as U-boats, aimed to impose a counter-blockade. It was difficult for underwater vessels to stop and search ships, so the U-boats planned to sink them without warning. For this reason, Germany declared its intention to attack only enemy, not neutral, shipping. However, when a U-boat torpedoed the British ship *Lusitania* on 7 May 1915, 128 American passengers drowned. This led to outcry across the USA and President Woodrow Wilson threatened war.

Germany could not risk the USA joining the Allies. It also knew that with just 22 submarines, it could never make the counter-blockade fully effective. So it changed its strategy. U-boats began to surface in order to inspect ships in the blockade zone, seizing cargoes when it was considered necessary. However, German methods altered again in 1917 (see pages 40-1).

In this photograph, which dates from 1916, German sailors stand on top of a U-boat that has come to the surface. In 1917, the U-boat campaign increased dramatically (see page 40).

During the First World War, Martin Niemöller served on German U-boats. He later became a Protestant minister who made a stand against Adolf Hitler and spent the Second World War in a concentration camp. This description of a U-boat attack in spring 1916 appears in his autobiography *From U-boat to Concentration Camp* (1939).

U-boats were fitted with deck guns.

Inverlyon is the name of the ship that the U-boat had stopped.

The German government placed this advertisement in the *New York World* newspaper on 1 May 1915, the day the *Lusitania* set sail from the USA. Few passengers believed that Germany would target a liner. A total of 1200 people died when the ship was hit six days later.

THE BATTLE OF JUTLAND

The dreadnoughts met in one major battle, which was triggered by the actions of German naval chief Admiral Reinhard Scheer. On 31 May 1916, Scheer sent battle cruisers to the seas off Jutland, a Danish peninsula. He hoped that the British would send ships of the same size in response. German dreadnoughts would then steam in to destroy the British vessels. However, the Royal Navy learned of Scheer's plans. It sent battle cruisers from Rosyth, as he was expecting. But it also sent dreadnoughts from Scapa Flow. The six-hour battle that followed was indecisive, but afterwards the German dreadnoughts returned to their ports for good.

Hove to means 'came to a stop'.

...on the afternoon of the 11th [April], we approached a large sailing vessel, which **hove to** at our warning shot, her crew taking to the boats, while we tried to sink her by **gunfire**. It was a difficult job, as the sea kept breaking right over the gun's crew, and... Seaman Pehrson was washed overboard when his lifebelt carried away. All attempts to pick him up... failed... When the **Inverlyon** was finally sunk, after a couple of dozen hits, none of us could rejoice at this first success.

The sinking of the *Lusitania*

Travellers intending to embark on the Atlantic voyage are reminded that a state of war exists between Germany and her allies; that the zone of war includes the waters adjacent to the British Isles; that, in accordance with formal notice given by the Imperial German Government, vessels flying the flag of Great Britain, or of any of her allies, are liable to destruction in those waters and that travellers sailing in the war zone on ships of Great Britain or her allies do so at their own risk.

THE HOME FRONTS

Civilian life was transformed by the First World War and people had no choice but to adapt. They believed that they were fighting for victory, not on the Eastern and Western battle fronts, but on the home front.

Much of civilian life in Britain was controlled by the Defence of the Realm Act (DORA), passed on 8 August 1914. It granted the government emergency powers, for example to court-martial people who put the country's security at risk and to take over factories for munitions production. DORA was regularly extended. It eventually allowed the government to use private land for crop-growing, to increase working hours, to censor newspapers, and much more.

Government interference was not the only consequence of the war for British civilians. Women took on many new roles (see pages 30-1). Everyone paid higher taxes to fund the fighting,

Civilians line up to receive mutton stew, toad-in-the-hole, puddings and other food at this communal kitchen in Hammersmith, London in 1917.

and everyone suffered food shortages. These shortages worsened in 1917 when Germany began unrestricted submarine warfare. Rationing was introduced in 1918.

Many French civilians had to endure even worse conditions, as about 12 per cent of their land was either occupied or in use as a battlefield. In addition, conscription meant that almost every man aged 18 to 47 was away at the front. (Britain introduced conscription in 1916 – see page 35.) As in Britain, serious food supply problems began in 1917. Rationing, introduced in 1914, grew ever more strict, and prices soared.

In Germany, conscription sent millions of men to the trenches in 1914. Once the German government realised the conflict would not be over quickly, it mobilised the civilian population for war, too. Much of this workforce produced arms and ammunition.

Heavy guns in production at the giant Krupp Works in Essen, Germany (see page 9).

As a result of the British blockade (see page 26), Germany experienced food shortages almost from the start of the war. Rationing began in 1915. By winter 1916, people in Germany were starving. Forced employment, hunger and military failure changed the character of the German home front, as early patriotism turned to great bitterness (see pages 54-5).

In Russia, lack of food, harsh conditions in munitions factories and humiliation in battle also led to serious unrest. Tsar Nicholas II and his wife Alexandra proved unable to deal with the problems. Revolution and an early exit from the war followed (see pages 46-7).

TOTAL WAR

Until 1914, wars were usually confined to battlefields. Though changed, life elsewhere in the participating countries was not utterly transformed. The First World War was different. Civilian workers produced deadly armaments on a massive scale. Governments and, especially in Germany, the army took control of daily life. Air raids (see pages 36-7) brought the conflict to the home fronts, and high death rates in battle left almost every family in mourning. German general Erich Ludendorff coined a term for this new phenomenon – total war.

 In this second extract from his autobiography, Robert Graves (see page 19) describes the effects of rationing on his London wedding.

Nancy and I were married in January 1918 at St James's Church, Piccadilly... At this stage of the war, sugar could not be got except in the form of rations. There was a three-tiered wedding-cake and the Nicholsons had been saving up their sugar and butter cards for a month to make it taste like a real one; but when George Mallory lifted off the plaster-case of imitation icing, a sigh of disappointment rose from the guests.

The government issued people with ration books. They contained coupons that were detached by the shop-owner every time a purchase was made. They could also be used in restaurants.

British ration books

Germans queuing for food in 1915

 In Germany, the situation was more serious than in the UK. About 750,000 Germans died of starvation during the war. Evelyn, Princess Blücher (see page 13), wrote this account of hunger on the German home front.

KRIEBLOWITZ, January 1917.—We are all growing thinner every day, and the rounded contours of the German nation have become a legend of the past. We are all gaunt and bony now, and have dark shadows round our eyes, and our thoughts are chiefly taken up with wondering what our next meal will be, and dreaming of the good things that once existed.

WOMEN AT WAR

This French magazine dates from 1916. The cover illustration contrasts the hat-making and other light work done by women before the war with the heavy industrial work that they carried out during the war.

Women's lives altered profoundly in the First World War. Many took on traditional male roles at home, while some ventured into war zones.

Before the war, about 25 per cent of Britain's 23.7 million women worked outside the home. Most of the rest were full-time wives and mothers. However, as men went to fight, and especially after conscription began in 1916, women filled the jobs that soldiers left behind. They also took on new jobs created by the demands of war. Women worked in munitions factories, as well as a wide range of other occupations, from printer to bus conductor. Many also joined the Women's Land Army, founded in 1916, and spent the war on the nation's farms.

Thousands of British women went out to the fronts. Some, mainly from the upper classes, belonged to the First Aid Nursing Yeomanry (FANY). Most of its members served as ambulance drivers. Women who enrolled in the Voluntary Aid Detachment (VAD) carried out a huge variety of tasks, from nursing with the Red Cross to cooking. In 1917, the government set up branches of the army, navy and air force for women, but their members did not take part in combat.

French women worked in factories, fields and offices throughout the war. By mid-1915, 30,000 women were making munitions in France. In 1916, a new law forbade employers to hire men for jobs that women could do. A Committee on Female

Many British women worked as wartime bus conductors.

Labour was also established to monitor women's working conditions. French women also served as nurses, at home and on the battlefield.

Germany did not allow women to go to the front. However, at home they turned their hands to almost everything, from the production of ammunition to building an underground train system in Berlin. The National Women's Service League organised nurseries to look after children while women worked.

By the end of the war, women were more confident of their own abilities than ever before. Their demands for the right to vote grew louder. British women got the vote in 1918 and German women in 1919, but their French counterparts had to wait until 1945. However, as returning soldiers reclaimed their jobs, thousands of women everywhere had to give up their working lives.

EDITH CAVELL

In 1914, English nurse Edith Cavell was matron of a Red Cross hospital in Brussels. When the Germans occupied the city during their invasion of Belgium, she helped Allied soldiers escape into neutral Holland. The Germans caught her and sentenced her to death. Before she was killed by firing squad in October 1915, she said: "Standing, as I do, in the view of God and eternity, I realise that patriotism is not enough. I must have no hatred or bitterness towards anyone." She became a national heroine and helped to alter people's view of women at war.

Edith Cavell in the garden of her Brussels home in 1915

Maria Botchkareva, known as Yashka, was allowed to join the Russian army in 1914. In 1917, she set up the all-female 'Battalion of Death'. This extract from her autobiography, *Yashka: My Life as Peasant, Exile and Soldier* (1919), describes some incidents from the unit's early days.

I marched the recruits to four barbers' shops, where... a number of barbers cut short the hair of one woman after another... The same afternoon my soldiers received their first lessons... and the drilling went on without interference. Giggling was strictly forbidden... One day... **Mrs Pankhurst** was introduced to me, and I ordered the Battalion to salute the eminent visitor who had done so much for women and her country. Mrs Pankhurst became a frequent visitor to the Battalion, watching it with deep interest as it grew into a well-disciplined military unit.

Mrs Emmeline Pankhurst was a leader of the British 'Votes for Women' campaign.

Maria Botchkareva

1916

VERDUN

In 1916, battles on the Western Front reached new heights of horror. The first major offensive was launched by the Germans against the French.

Erich von Falkenhayn (see page 16) planned the new attack, codenamed *Gericht*. His aim was to crush the spirit of the French army. For this reason, he chose Verdun as the battle site – the capture of its forts had been a bitter blow to the French in the 1870-1 war (see page 9). He reasoned that if France collapsed, Britain would choose to start peace negotiations rather than continue alone.

Meanwhile the French commander, General Joffre, was planning a joint Franco-British attack on the Somme (see pages 34-5). So while Germany was preparing a force of 140,000 for the Verdun offensive, French troops and guns were moving away. Despite warnings, Joffre refused to recognise Verdun's importance or strengthen its defences.

The devastating German bombardment began on 21 February. Howitzers and other artillery rained down shells. As the German soldiers advanced, they unleashed phosgene gas and used flame-throwers for the first time. On 25 February, they captured Fort Douaumont, near Verdun, in three-quarters of an hour.

At this moment of crisis, Joffre called on General Henri Philippe Pétain for assistance. Pétain took control at Verdun, declaring: "They [the Germans] shall not pass." Then he set about turning his downcast, freezing troops, into a defensive machine. Soon the French artillery was responding to heavy German bombardments with equal ferocity. Pétain also improved the only French supply route, the so-called 'Sacred Way'.

THE WESTERN FRONT 1916-17

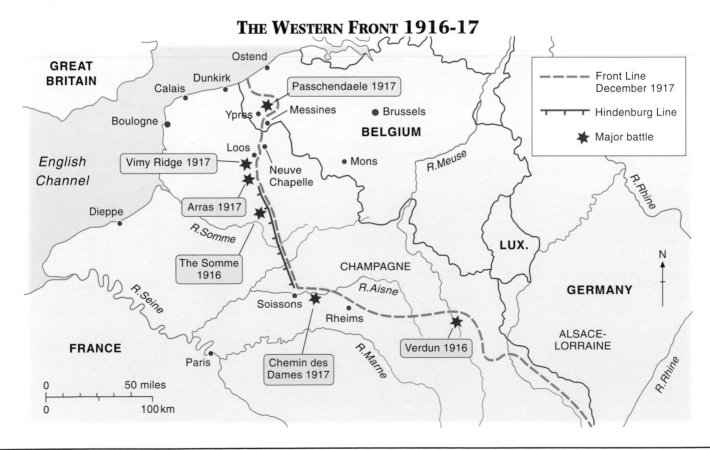

Members of a small French artillery unit at Verdun. Their quick-firing gun launched huge shells towards the enemy lines.

By 1916, the Russian army had regrouped after the disastrous retreat of the previous year (see page 25). Its commanders planned an attack in July, to coincide with the Allied offensive on the Somme. But by June, France was in trouble at Verdun and Italy was under pressure on its Austro-Hungarian border. Both asked Russia for help. So on 4 June, General Alexei Brusilov launched surprise attacks against the Austrian army on the Eastern Front. The Austrians were driven back, but the Germans came to their aid. Romania, which joined the Allies in August, tried to help Russia, but was swiftly defeated by Germany. By September, Russia had retreated and lost one million men.

Pétain's determination was matched by von Falkenhayn's. As a result, the fighting spiralled out of control. The Germans captured Fort Vaux, 3km from Verdun, on 7 June. However, as they moved towards the town itself, thousands of German troops had to leave for Russia (see box). Soon after, the British attacked on the Somme, diverting more German resources. Von Falkenhayn had missed his opportunity.

The fighting still continued, but with less intensity. Paul von Hindenburg took over from von Falkenhayn in August. In October, a French offensive recaptured Forts Douaumont and Vaux. By the time the battle ended in December, the front had returned almost to its original position and the toll of dead and wounded was nearly one million.

Verdun was the longest battle of the First World War. About 40 million artillery shells were fired as one bombardment followed after another. Henri Desagneaux (see page 13) served as a commander in the front line for two weeks. Here he describes the events of 17 June.

One cannot imagine what the simple phrase of an official statement like 'We have recaptured a trench' really means! The attack is prepared from 4 to 9 o'clock; all guns firing together. The Germans fire non-stop, **ammunition dumps** blow up... The wounded from this morning's attack are beginning to arrive, we learn what happened: our artillery fired too short and demolished our front line trench...When we attacked the Germans let us advance to 15 metres and then caught us in a hail of machine-gunfire. We succeeded in capturing several parts of the trench but couldn't hold them... At nightfall, the dead arrive on stretchers at the cemetery... Major Payen, his head red with blood; Major Cormouls, black with smoke, still others unrecognizable and often in pieces.

An **ammunition dump** was a place where ammunition was stored.

THE SOMME

By July 1916, the date of the Somme offensive, France was in dire trouble at Verdun. As a result, it could not send the agreed 40 troop divisions to the new battleground. Instead it sent five, while Britain initially supplied 14. But General Sir Douglas Haig (see page 25) still believed that an all-out 'push' would produce the vital break in the German lines.

General Haig believed in offensive warfare and in the power of mounted troops. He planned to use both on the Somme, pushing infantry (footsoldiers) forwards until the enemy cracked, then sending in cavalry. In fact, such 19th-century tactics were no match for 20th-century military technology.

The British soldiers, many of them inexperienced volunteers, faced a daunting task. The Germans were on high ground, so they could defend their lines

British painter Paul Nash became a soldier in 1914 and an official war artist in 1916. His painting of trench warfare in winter is called *Over the Top*. Nash was also an official artist in the Second World War.

General Sir Douglas Haig

relatively easily. They also had a good view of enemy activity below. The German trenches were solidly built with deep dugouts that protected troops during bombardments.

The British began their bombardment on 23 June and pounded the Germans with artillery for a week. The aim was to destroy the German front-line trenches and barbed wire before the advance. However, the guns could not wipe out the Germans' deep dugouts, and shrapnel shells were ineffective against the barbed wire. Nevertheless, the infantry attack began on 1 July.

As the lines of British soldiers went over the top, German machine-gunners, sheltered in dugouts, mowed them down. The German artillery joined the fray,

too. Soon No Man's Land was littered with corpses and injured men crying out in pain. About 120,000 men attacked on that first day. By the end of the day, about 20,000 were dead and 40,000 wounded, missing or prisoners of the Germans.

Haig forged ahead with his plan regardless, and the number of deaths mounted. Germans fell in their thousands, too. On 15 September, the Allies used tanks in battle for the first time. Some broke down. The others moved so slowly that the Germans could target them with ease. An Allied attack in November failed and the battle drifted to its end. Total casualties in the Somme were over one million, about 60 per cent of them Allied troops. Britain had won about 12km of land.

Captain R.J. Trousdell of the Royal Irish Fusiliers wrote this description of the Somme battle area.

In the open, no sign of vegetation was visible: shell craters literally overlapped over square miles – gashes in the torn surface, more or less continuous and deeper than the rest – indicated trenches, and in these our troops managed to exist, shelled day and night until they went forward to the attack or were replaced by other troops... Thickly timbered woods were reduced to a few gaunt and splintered trunks. Stripped of every leaf and twig – without undergrowth – almost without roots. Villages disappeared as though they had never been...

Shells have all but destroyed this wood on the Somme battlefield.

Many Australians fought on the Somme. In this poem, Australian soldier Vance Palmer writes about his inability to forget the experience.

Aeroplanes flew over the battlefield (see pages 36-7).

Will they never fade or pass –
The mud, and the misty figures endlessly coming
In file through the foul morass,
And the grey flood-water lipping the reeds and grass,
And the **steel wings drumming**?
...
I have returned to these;
The farm, and kindly Bush, and the young calves lowing;
But all that my mind sees
Is a quaking bog in a mist – stark, snapped trees,
And the **dark Somme flowing.**

The Somme area is named after the river that runs through it.

THE MILITARY SERVICE ACT

Until 1916, the British army consisted of regular (career) soldiers and the three million volunteers recruited by Lord Kitchener (see page 17). However, heavy losses meant that many more men were needed. So in January 1916, the Military Service Act was passed. It introduced conscription – compulsory military service – for single men aged 18 to 41. In May, married men were called up, too. The age limit was also gradually raised to 50. Some men were exempted from conscription. They included conscientious objectors, who often faced hostility and imprisonment.

THE WAR IN THE AIR

British observers in a kite balloon observe enemy activity on the Western Front. Kite balloons were tethered to the ground, but could rise to 1800m.

Both the Allies and the Central Powers used aircraft from the beginning of the First World War. However, it was not until later that aeroplanes began to play a substantial part in the conflict.

At the start of the war, aeroplanes were sent out to observe enemy lines and detect troop movements and trench locations. The artillery used information from aerial observers to target their guns. No military leader yet thought of planes as fighting machines.

Change came after both sides sent up aeroplanes to shoot down reconnaissance aircraft. The pilots fixed machine-guns on their planes in order to attack the enemy. But if the guns fired forwards, there was a risk of hitting the propellers. In 1915, Frenchman Roland Garros invented a device to make the guns fire only when the propellers were turned away. The Germans shot Garros down, and their designer Anthony Fokker improved his invention. After German planes were fitted with the new 'interrupter gear', the Allies made their own interrupter system.

From 1915 onwards, fighter planes armed with this new technology engaged in sky duels over the trenches. The era of the daredevil flying aces had begun.

Air tactics changed as the war continued, and as better planes were developed. The aim of the Allied squadrons was to keep certain areas clear of enemy aircraft by mounting regular patrols. German squadrons operated the 'circus system', moving to wherever the need was greatest. Formation-fighting took over from individual combat, and planes began to attack ground targets, such as trenches.

Aircraft were also used to bomb areas far from the fronts. German Zeppelin airships attacked civilian targets in Britain,

This painting shows an aerial dogfight between German and British biplanes. The German aircraft are marked with black crosses, the British with red, white and blue bull's-eye symbols.

France and elsewhere from 1914. The raids declined after 1916 as the Allies began to shoot down the hydrogen-filled ships with incendiary bullets. From 1917, Allied bombers regularly attacked factories and mines in Germany, while German Gotha bombers raided British cities. By 1918, aircraft were recognised as a powerful means of waging war.

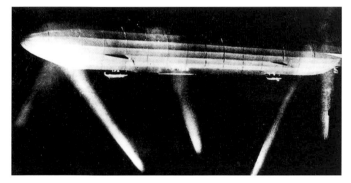

Searchlights pick out a huge German Zeppelin as it prepares to bomb the British mainland during a night-time raid.

THE ROYAL AIR FORCE

When the war began, Britain had two airborne fighting forces. The Royal Flying Corps was part of the army and the Royal Naval Air Service part of the navy. As the importance of airpower increased, the need for change became clear. Major-General Sir Hugh Trenchard, head of the Royal Flying Corps, did not want the army to lose control of its air force. But he was persuaded to take on the task of creating a unified service. The Royal Air Force was formed in April 1918.

The German 'Red Baron' (see document) was the most successful flying ace. He shot down 80 planes before he was brought down in 1918.

The 'Red Baron', Manfred von Richthofen, was so called because his Fokker plane was painted red. During the war, von Richthofen kept a diary. It was published after his death, with a selection of his letters. This extract is taken from one of the letters.

Before Verdun, 3 May 1916
Very sincere thanks for your kind wishes on my birthday, which I spent very pleasantly here. In the morning I had three very nerve-wracking aerial combats, and in the evening I sat with Zeumer, my first pilot, until one o'clock in the morning with a bowl of punch under a blossoming apple tree. I feel very content with my new occupation as a fighter pilot; I believe that no post in the war is as attractive as this one.

The full name of the British pilot who wrote this extract is not known. Dated August 1917, his view of the war in the air is quite different from that of the Red Baron (above).

The flying job is rotten for one's nerve, and although one is supposed to last 6 months with a fortnight's leave half way, quite a lot of people's nerve completely conks out after 4 or 4½... No one can imagine the strain of 2½ hours over the line. Firstly one has to keep one's place in the formation... then one has to watch the leader, who does all the scientific dodging of Archie... Then there's every single machine in the sky to be suspicious about, until you've proved it isn't a Hun.

Archie is slang for anti-aircraft gunfire from the ground.

Hun is an impolite word for 'German'.

PROPAGANDA AND CENSORSHIP

Propaganda (biased information designed to support a particular cause) and censorship (the suppression of information) were widely used during the First World War. Governments, armies and media on both sides grew increasingly reliant on them as the conflict progressed.

Propaganda began with the war. Newspapers and the general public spread rumours that the enemy's troops were evil and had committed atrocities, such as cutting off dead soldiers' feet. Enemy incompetence was another favourite topic. The French press announced that German shells were made of cardboard. At the same time, people glorified their own troops'

bravery. The troops themselves were not impressed by such stories. Troops at the fronts often felt closer to their enemies nearby, who knew the truth, than to misinformed people at home.

The nature of government news censorship varied from country to country. The War Press Office in Germany exercised strict control, enforced by the army. The French authorities did not permit the lists of war dead and wounded to be published, but provided rose-tinted stories of their own. In Britain, a member of Lord Kitchener's staff wrote the official war reports. Kitchener then had to approve them before they were sent out to the newspapers. From May 1915,

This poster advertises Liberty Bonds, certificates of debt sold by the American government to pay for the war. By showing an evil-looking German (Hun) soldier, it also acts as anti-German propaganda.

some British journalists were allowed to join troops at the front and send reports home.

The propaganda war increased in 1916, when cinema took on an important role. A film called *The Battle of the Somme* was made on the battlefield while the fighting was still under way. Its scenes of brave British troops were intended to encourage the public at home. However, many people were shocked by the violence – even though it did not begin to match the awful reality. German commander Erich Ludendorff supported the making of propaganda news films from 1917. They showed favourable images of Germany's troops at the fronts and people flocked to watch them.

British comedy actor Charlie Chaplin starred in a silent propaganda film called *Shoulder Arms* (1918). In it, he won the war on his own!

This letter, dated 1916, was written by a British soldier. Information that might have been of use to the enemy has been crossed out by the censor.

THE HINDENBURG CULT

An unusual propaganda scheme was developed by German military officials to cover up the failure of the Schlieffen Plan (see page 12). Playing on the public's wish to idolise its soldiers, they encouraged the hero-worship of a particular military leader. This was Paul von Hindenburg, one of the commanders responsible for German victory at Tannenberg (see page 14).

A vast statue of Hindenburg was built in Berlin's Tiergarten park. People paid for the privilege of banging nails into the statue. This was supposed to make Hindenburg an even stronger 'Iron Man'. The money helped to pay for the war.

Crowds flock around the statue of Hindenburg in Berlin, while a military band plays to entertain them.

Propaganda leaflets dropped by aeroplanes and airships over the trenches were designed to demoralise the enemy. These leaflets generally informed troops that defeat was close and resistance useless. This is the text of a leaflet that the Germans dropped over American lines in 1918, a year after the USA joined the Allies.

NEVER SAY DIE!
Don't die until you have to!
What business have you to die for France, for Alsace-Lorraine, or for England in France?
Isn't it better anyhow to live than to die, no matter for how "glorious" a cause? Isn't it better to live and come back to the old folks at home, than to rot in the shell holes and trenches of France?
If you surrender to us, we will treat you fair enough.
Why run any more chances than you have to?
You might as well be a free boarder in Germany till the war is over.
YOU DON'T WANT TO DIE TILL YOU HAVE TO!

CHAPTER 5

1917
ENTER THE USA

The great Western Front confrontations of 1916 – Verdun and the Somme – had no real victors. They were classic battles of attrition in which each side tried to win simply by inflicting high casualties on the other. By 1917, it was clear that this strategy had failed. Erich Ludendorff, who now controlled the German armed forces together with Paul von Hindenburg, changed tactics in the trenches (see pages 42-3). He also decided that the war could only be won at sea.

On 31 January 1917, Germany declared unrestricted submarine warfare. All shipping in the Atlantic war zone, neutral as well as Allied, was to be sunk. By taking this extreme measure, Germany hoped to starve Britain, force the Allies into peace negotiations and bring the war to a swift end. It had reason to hope for success because it had far more U-boats – well over 200 – than in 1915 (see pages 26-7).

The American president, Woodrow Wilson, was appalled by the German move and immediately broke off diplomatic relations. However, he still wanted to continue the US policy of isolationism. Then, events forced his hand. The British intercepted a telegram sent by the German Foreign Secretary, Arthur Zimmermann, to the German ambassador in Mexico. It said that if Woodrow Wilson declared war, Germany would help Mexico regain its former territory in New Mexico, Texas and Arizona from the USA. In return, Germany would expect Mexican support.

The telegram appeared in American newspapers and provoked great anger. U-boats then sank seven American ships. Woodrow Wilson could hold back

This idealistic illustration of soldiers leaving for the war appeared on the cover of an American children's magazine in 1918.

President Woodrow Wilson reads the USA's declaration of war to Congress (the American parliament) on 6 April 1917.

American troops land at St-Nazaire on the French coast in June 1917.

THE US ARMY

Before it entered the war, the US Army had only about 200,000 members. By the end of the conflict, about two million Americans, including 200,000 African-Americans, were serving in Europe. They brought little experience of trench warfare to the fronts and were largely dependent on the other Allies for weapons and equipment. However, they made a major contribution to the Allied victory (see pages 52-3).

no longer. On 6 April 1917, he declared war. In May, the Selective Service Act made it compulsory for all American men aged 21 to 30 to join the armed forces (the age range later became 18 to 45). General John Pershing was put in charge of the American Expeditionary Force and the first troops reached France in June.

Meanwhile, the U-boat campaign was taking its toll. By spring 1917, the Germans were destroying about 800 vessels each month. Ships from many countries refused even to approach Britain, so its stocks of food and other goods were dwindling fast. David Lloyd George, who had become British prime minister in 1916, devised a solution. From April, merchant ships travelled in convoys (groups) of about 40, flanked by warship escorts. The plan worked. Over the next six months, only 24 from a total of 1500 ships bound for Britain were sunk.

This extract comes from a letter written by Sergeant Phelps Harding, whose 306th Infantry Regiment formed part of the American Expeditionary Force.

**Camp Upton, N.Y.,
29 March, 1918**

Dear Dad,
I just wrote Mother that the regiment is almost ready to leave for France... This letter is addressed to you... to avoid Mother seeing it. I simply want to tell you that we were secretly... practically given our preference as to whether we would rather serve here or abroad... Don't tell Mother that I had an opportunity to stay here, for I know that it would make her feel badly that I did not stay. I am just telling you so that if anything should happen to me you will know that I met the danger of my own free will, and with a full knowledge of what to expect in the fighting on the other side. I'm mighty glad I have the chance to go over and do my share – and I know you are glad to have me go...

THE NIVELLE OFFENSIVE

In December 1916, General Robert Nivelle replaced General Joffre as the French Chief of Staff. Nivelle planned to launch a new Allied offensive in 1917 that would finally break the Western Front stalemate.

Erich Ludendorff had decided on the opposite approach. He had already put Germany on the *offensive* at sea (see pages 40-1). On the Western Front he wanted to strengthen Germany's *defensive* position. So troops were ordered to withdraw about 30km to the east and build the Hindenburg Line (see map page 32). A complex system of barbed wire, machine-gun emplacements and dugouts stretched for many kilometres along the line and up to 16km back from it. Its purpose was to keep the enemy at bay.

Nivelle's offensive was to begin in Champagne in mid-April. On 9 April, the British,

The Germans spent months building strong, deep trenches like this along the Hindenburg Line. Troops withdrew to the line in March 1917.

Canadians and Australians launched a smaller attack at Arras, to the north. The aim was to keep the Germans busy while the main preparations continued elsewhere. At first all went well. The Allies advanced about 5km and the Canadians captured the

area of high ground known as Vimy Ridge. But the Germans fought back strongly and the battle petered out on 17 May.

The main attack, launched on 16 April, took place in an area known as the Chemin des Dames, near Rheims. But the Germans had learned of the French plan in advance from a captured soldier and were fully prepared. During the first two days of the offensive, French soldiers advanced into a torrent of machine-gun bullets. It was soon clear that no breakthrough was possible, but Nivelle continued the attack. After two weeks, the French had advanced about half a kilometre. Casualty figures had reached 250,000.

Canadian troops move towards Vimy Ridge. They were led by General Sir Julian Byng, who later became Governor-General of Canada.

The pointless slaughter and Nivelle's persistence – the offensive continued into May – led to mutiny among French troops. Reserves due on the front lines simply refused to move, and front-line troops refused to attack. Eventually about half a million men joined the protests. Calm returned when Nivelle was replaced by General Pétain. He promised the troops an end to huge, unwinnable offensives, reminded them that American help was on the way and improved the conditions in which they lived and fought.

British soldiers prepare for the Battle of Arras. The men at the front are observing the enemy using a periscope and binoculars. The others are passing information on to troops elsewhere using a field telephone.

In Arras, Allied troops extended an existing cave system under the city to provide shelter and a way of reaching German lines without exposing themselves to gunfire. Brigadier-General Douglas, Lord Loch wrote this account of the caves.

The old French built their towns by quarrying down till they came to the hard chalk and then dug it out. This has made huge caves. We joined them up and made entrances etc. Lit them by electric light. Made cook houses – Divisional and Brigade headquarters etc., etc. On the day of the attack you could walk underground from the centre of Arras to the German front line. The last 150 feet we blew out at **zero hour**. We consequently had communication trenches across No Man's Land in under half an hour.

Zero hour means the hour when the attack began.

PRISONERS OF WAR

The soldier who revealed the Nivelle Offensive details to the Germans was one of about eight million prisoners taken in the First World War. After an attack, captured men were usually herded together in cages, then moved to prison camps. After a period of questioning, they were often sent out to work, for example on farms. Conditions were poor. On the Eastern Front, many prisoners caught typhoid.

This illustration dates from 1917 and shows German prisoners behind the barbed wire fencing of a French prisoner-of-war camp.

PASSCHENDAELE

The French mutiny came to an end in June. As Pétain had promised, France launched no more major attacks during the First World War. However, Haig began to argue that one last, British-led push could bring the Germans to their knees. The location that he favoured for the attempt was Ypres (see pages 16 and 24-5).

Ypres was in a salient – a bulge in the front line surrounded by enemy-held land. Despite the difficulty of attacking in such an area, Haig wanted to break out of the salient and sweep forwards to the Belgian ports that the Germans were using as submarine bases. British prime minister Lloyd George had grave doubts about the plan. However, Haig pointed out that the German forces were weaker than in the past, while the British had new weapons, aircraft and tanks, better battle techniques and more accurate aerial photographs.

On 7 June 1917, before the main attack began, Allied troops led by General Sir Herbert Plumer used underground mines to seize the Messines Ridge. This was an area of high ground near Ypres that gave the Germans a clear view of the enemy. The operation was brilliantly executed. But instead of moving swiftly to take advantage of German confusion, the Allies waited seven weeks before launching the offensive.

The Third Battle of Ypres began on 31 July 1917. Rain soon began to fall in sheets and the preliminary bombardment – the biggest yet – hurled over 4.5 million shells into the battleground mud. Troops advanced through a swamp. Progress was slow throughout August and losses heavy. However, during a dry spell in September, Anzac and British troops captured Menin Road Ridge, Polygon Wood and Broodseinde.

Torrential rain fell again in October and men and horses

Stretcher-bearers in the mud at Passchendaele in 1917. Torrential rain turned the battlefield into a lethal quagmire.

drowned in the mud. Despite the conditions, troops struggled on. Canadians took the village of Passchendaele, after which the battle is now named, on 6 November. Haig then stopped the offensive. The Allies had advanced 10km into the salient, leaving themselves more exposed. Over 400,000 had died. Reeling from the worst horror yet, men almost lost hope.

The Battle of Cambrai, which began about 80km south of Ypres on 28 November, gave the Allies a small boost. About 400 tanks of a new type known as Mark IV smashed through German lines and advanced 8km. However, the Germans quickly regained the ground.

A Mark IV tank in action at Cambrai. The battle was such a success for the Allies that church bells in London were rung to celebrate.

The Battle of Passchendaele was a disaster. However, in his papers Field Marshal Haig recalls that he received the following congratulatory telegram from the British government on 16 October 1917.

The War Cabinet desire to congratulate you and the troops under your command upon the achievements of the British Armies in Flanders in the great battle which has been raging since July 31st. Starting from positions in which every advantage rested with the enemy and, hampered and delayed from time to time by most unfavourable weather, you and your men have nevertheless continuously driven the enemy back with such skill, courage, and **pertinacity**, as have commanded the grateful admiration of the peoples of the British Empire and filled the enemy with alarm...

Pertinacity means 'determination'.

THE BATTLE OF CAPORETTO

Italy had been struggling against the Austro-Hungarians on its border since 1915 (see page 25). Much of the fighting took place in the Alps. The two sides were evenly balanced and by 1917 neither had achieved a decisive victory. Then Erich Ludendorff sent in German troops to help the Austro-Hungarians and a joint attack was launched at Caporetto on 24 October. Italy suffered a major defeat and its army retreated over 100km. British and French troops rushed to the rescue (see page 55).

EXIT RUSSIA

The First World War had shamed Russia's armies. They had been crushed at Tannenberg in 1914, driven out of Poland in 1915, and forced to retreat after the Brusilov Offensive of 1916. Comfort was not to be found at home, where food shortages were leading to starvation, inflation was soaring and industrial unrest was increasing.

Tsar Nicholas II had already survived one revolution, in 1905. In March 1917, he came under threat again. Women queuing for food in Russia's capital, Petrograd (present-day St Petersburg), began to riot. Unrest spread and protesters took to the streets. The tsar ordered the army to shoot into the

THE EASTERN FRONT 1917-18

Baltic Sea

• Moscow

Riga

Area occupied under Treaty of Brest-Litovsk, March 1918

Armistice Line

N

GERMANY

0   200 miles
0   300 km

Brest-Litovsk

• Warsaw

Failed Russian offensive 1917

Kiev

R U S S I A

POLAND

R.Dnieper

GALICIA

UKRAINE

AUSTRIA-HUNGARY

Odessa

CRIMEA

ROMANIA

Black Sea

Tsar Nicholas II with three of his daughters. He, his wife Alexandra and their five children were all executed by revolutionaries on 16 July 1918.

crowds. However, many ordinary soldiers simply refused to fire.

The tsar now realised that change was inevitable. He set up a provisional government, headed by Prince Lvov, to take control of the country. Then, on 17 March, he abdicated. Prince Lvov and his ministers had to decide whether Russia should withdraw from the war. The provisional government did not want to abandon its allies, so it chose to continue.

Soldiers were now even more reluctant to fight. Many began to support the revolutionaries who were campaigning for an immediate end to the war. These men had set up workers' committees, known as *soviets*, right across the country, and their power was growing. The Germans decided to exploit this

situation. They allowed Vladimir Lenin, leader of the revolutionary Bolshevik Party, to return by train to Russia from Switzerland via Germany. He arrived in April.

The situation grew steadily worse for the provisional government. In June its new leader, Alexander Kerensky, ordered an offensive against Germany. It was a total failure and German troops advanced east. The Petrograd soviet, headed by Lenin's fellow Bolshevik, Leon Trotsky, believed that the time had come to seize power. On 6 November, Trotsky launched the revolution. Bolshevik forces took over the city and the government fled.

Lenin became leader of the new Russia and began talks with Germany to end his country's participation in the First World

War. The ceasefire began on 3 December 1917. Leon Trotsky, now foreign minister, started negotiations to decide the peace terms. The Treaty of Brest-Litovsk, signed in March 1918, brought more humiliation to Russia. It was forced to sign away vast areas of land (see map).

In this scene from the 1917 revolution, Bolsheviks in Petrograd take aim at government supporters.

VLADIMIR LENIN

Vladimir Ilyich Lenin trained as a lawyer and while still a young man became a follower of the German philosopher Karl Marx. The Russian government punished him for spreading Marxist political ideas by sending him to Siberia in 1895. He was released in 1900, and five years later played an important part in the 1905 revolution. After its failure he was exiled to Switzerland, where he remained until the Germans returned him to Russia in 1917. Lenin ruled his country from the revolution until his death in 1924. His tomb is in Moscow's Red Square.

Lenin was a powerful speaker, as this Russian poster indicates. He used his skill to spread Communist ideas.

This is part of a speech that Lenin made to the Petrograd soviet on the day that the Bolsheviks seized the city.

Lenin is referring to the revolutions of 1905, March 1917 and November 1917.

Lenin believed in Marx's theory of revolutionary socialism. It teaches that the working class should overthrow the capitalist system, in which industry is privately owned, and replace it with a new system based on common ownership.

Proletarian means 'working class'.

From now on, a new phase in the history of Russia begins, and this, the third Russian revolution, should in the end lead to the victory of socialism. One of our urgent tasks is to put an immediate end to the war... We shall be helped in this by the world working-class movement, which is already beginning to develop in Italy, Britain and Germany. The proposal we make to international democracy for a just and immediate peace will everywhere awaken an ardent response among the international proletarian masses.

WAR IN THE MIDDLE EAST

Gallipoli (see pages 22-3) was not the only place where the Allies and Turks fought. They also clashed in Palestine and Mesopotamia (modern Iraq), both of which were then part of the Ottoman Empire. In 1917, as Russia was preparing to leave the war, Allied activity in the Middle East increased. This was because the Allies feared that Turkish troops who had been fighting the Russians would now move to the Middle East.

The Allies' interest in Palestine stemmed from their wish to protect the Suez Canal, a vital shipping link that cuts through Egypt to connect the Mediterranean and Red seas. The Turks attacked the canal in 1915. Throughout 1916, the British pushed them steadily back into Palestine, but were unable to defeat them outright. In early 1917, two more British attacks failed. Britain sent General Sir Edmund Allenby to lead a new offensive in June of the same year. The appointment was successful. The Palestinian towns of Gaza and Beersheba fell in October. Jerusalem surrendered on 9 December.

Allenby's offensive was backed by Arabs who wanted to throw off Turkish rule. They were led by Emir Feisal ibn Hussein, whose father was the

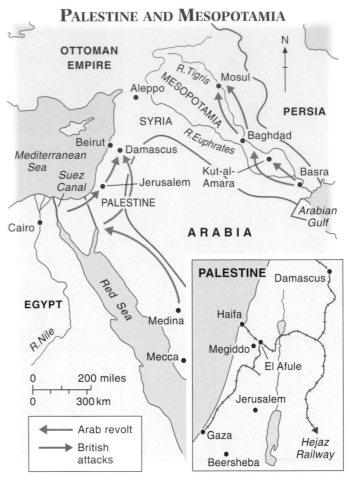

PALESTINE AND MESOPOTAMIA

Arab revolt
British attacks

General Sir Edmund Allenby

Sherif (governor) of Mecca. Feisal was supported by British army intelligence officer T.E. Lawrence, now known as Lawrence of Arabia (see document page 49). The two men organised the Arabs into highly effective guerrilla units that constantly harassed the Turks.

The British landed in Mesopotamia in November 1914. Troops arrived at the top of the Arabian Gulf and made their way north, but in December 1915 the Turks besieged them at Kut-al-Amara. Starvation forced a British surrender in April 1916. A renewed campaign in 1917 led to the fall of Baghdad in March. The British then continued north, taking Mosul in autumn 1918.

The Palestine campaign also ended in late 1918. In preparation for the final attack, the Arabs blew up parts of the Hejaz Railway, the Turks' supply line. Then on 19 September, Allenby's forces

Among the troops under Allenby's command were members of the Imperial Camel Corps. These soldiers came from many countries, including Britain, Australia, New Zealand, India and Egypt.

– British, French, Indians and Anzacs – struck at places along the line, including Megiddo and El Afule. Turkish forces collapsed and the Allies moved north, taking Damascus on 1 October. On 30 October, the Turks signed an armistice.

T.E. Lawrence and Emir Feisal had expected the Allies to reward their Arab supporters with independence once the Ottoman Empire was defeated. However, the British and French carved up its territory between them. In accordance with the British government's Balfour Declaration of 1917, Palestine later became a homeland for the Jews.

WAR IN AFRICA

In 1914, France and Britain both had large empires. They called on soldiers from many of their colonies, for example in Africa, to fight for the Allied cause. The Germans also had some African colonies, and First World War battles took place on their territory. Togoland surrendered to the Allies in August 1914, Southwest Africa in May 1915 and the Cameroons in February 1916. However, German forces in East Africa struggled on for four years, launching guerrilla raids over the Mozambique border until after the end of the war. They finally surrendered in November 1918.

Colonel T.E. Lawrence in Arab dress

 Thomas Edward (T.E.) Lawrence was a brilliant scholar. He spoke fluent Arabic and had a deep knowledge of Arab history.

In 1926, he published *The Seven Pillars of Wisdom*, a history of the Arab revolt. In this extract he explains why he abandoned British army uniform for Arab dress.

British army uniform is **khaki** (olive-brown) in colour.

Feisal came from Mecca, the holiest city of Islam. It is now in Saudi Arabia.

Suddenly Feisal asked me if I would wear Arab clothes like his own while in camp. I should find it better for my own part, since it was a comfortable dress in which to live Arab-fashion as we must do. Besides, the tribesmen would then understand how to take me. The only wearers of khaki in their experience had been Turkish officers, before whom they took up an instinctive defence. If I wore Meccan clothes, they would behave to me as though I were really one of the leaders; and I might slip in and out of Feisal's tent without making a sensation which he had to explain away each time to strangers.

1918

THE GERMAN OFFENSIVE

By 1918, the situation on the Western Front did not look good for the Allies. The Nivelle Offensive and Passchendaele (see pages 42-5) had been disasters. The Italians had been forced into retreat at Caporetto. Worse, about one million German reinforcements were moving in from the Eastern Front, which had closed down after Russia's withdrawal from the war. However, the Americans were also coming (see pages 40-1).

German commander Erich Ludendorff's scheme to end the war using submarines had failed, so he decided to risk an all-out land attack. Ludendorff believed that the sheer number of German troops made victory likely. To boost their chances, he introduced tactics that had proved their worth in Russia. Among them was the use of storm troopers. Armed with light machine-guns and flame-throwers, these soldiers acted independently and had a devastating effect.

The German offensive began in France on 21 March 1918. The aim was to hit the British hard at St Quentin on the Somme, separate them from the French and drive them out to the coast. The preliminary bombardment was short, but immensely powerful. Then the 750,000-strong infantry flooded forward. The war of movement returned as the Germans advanced 60km in a week. The British, who numbered only 300,000, were forced to retreat. Paris was under threat.

The Germans kept up the offensive pressure for four months. But, flaws in Ludendorff's scheme slowly emerged. The speed of the advance and the war of attrition in 1916 and 1917 had exhausted the troops. Food supplies could not keep up with the men. Much of the artillery had been left behind, so German bombardments grew lighter. Allied air attacks also began to bite. Finally, there was no one to replace the thousands who had died in the fighting.

In April 1918, French general Ferdinand Foch was made Commander-in-Chief of all the Allied forces. The Americans made their first attack of the war at Cantigny in May. At Belleau Wood in June, they forced the Germans out of a long-held position. Foch realised that Allied strength was growing, while Germany was fading fast. In July, he decided that the time for counter-attack had come.

THE WESTERN FRONT 1918

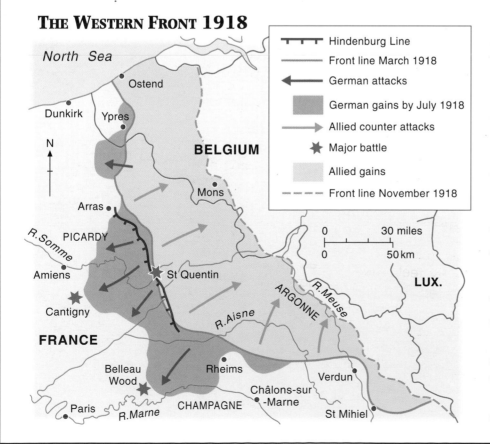

Legend:
- Hindenburg Line
- Front line March 1918
- German attacks
- German gains by July 1918
- Allied counter attacks
- Major battle
- Allied gains
- Front line November 1918

Map labels: North Sea, Ostend, Dunkirk, Ypres, Arras, Mons, BELGIUM, PICARDY, R. Somme, Amiens, St Quentin, Cantigny, FRANCE, Belleau Wood, Rheims, R. Aisne, ARGONNE, R. Meuse, Verdun, Châlons-sur-Marne, St Mihiel, LUX., CHAMPAGNE, Paris, R. Marne

0   30 miles
0   50 km

THE FOURTEEN POINTS

By early 1918, American president Woodrow Wilson was already planning for peace. On 8 January, he presented a programme of Fourteen Points (right) to the US Congress outlining his aims. This balanced list tried to be fair to all sides. Britain and France were wary of such idealism – they believed that Germany should be heavily punished for its aggression. However by the time the war was over, they had agreed that Wilson's Fourteen Points should provide the basis for the peace treaty discussions in Paris (see page 56).

 The German offensive on 21 March took place in fog, so the Allies were unable to see what was happening. Gas added to the confusion. Captain C.J. Lodge-Patch, a British medical officer, went out during the attack to warn his men to withdraw. Here he relates what happened next.

A **5.9** is a type of shell.

I felt it was... all up with me means 'I felt I was going to die'.

Program for the Peace of the World

By PRESIDENT WILSON, January 8, 1918

I. Open covenants of peace, openly arrived at, after which there shall be no private international understandings of any kind, but diplomacy shall proceed always frankly and in the public view.

II. Absolute freedom of navigation upon the seas, outside territorial waters, alike in peace and in war, except as the seas may be closed in whole or in part by international action for the enforcement of international covenants.

III. The removal, so far as possible, of all economic barriers and the establishment of an equality of trade conditions among all the nations consenting to the peace and associating themselves for its maintenance.

IV. Adequate guarantees given and taken that national armaments will reduce to the lowest point consistent with domestic safety.

V. Free, open-minded, and absolutely impartial adjustment of all colonial claims, based upon a strict observance of the principle that in determining all such questions of sovereignty the interests of the population concerned must have equal weight with the equitable claims of the government whose title is to be determined.

VI. The evacuation of all Russian territory and such a settlement of all questions affecting Russia as will secure the best and freest coöperation of the other nations of the world in obtaining for her an unhampered and unembarrassed opportunity for the independent determination of her own political development and national policy, and assure her of a sincere welcome into the society of free nations under institutions of her own choosing; and, more than a welcome, assistance also of every kind that she may need and may herself desire. The treatment accorded Russia by her sister nations in the months to come will be the acid test of their goodwill, of their comprehension of her needs as distinguished from their own interests, and of their intelligent and unselfish sympathy.

VII. Belgium, the whole world will agree, must be evacuated and restored, without any attempt to limit the sovereignty which she enjoys in common with all other free nations. No other single act will serve as this will serve to restore confidence among the nations in the law which they have themselves set and determined for the government of their relations with one another. Without this healing act the whole structure and validity of international law is forever impaired.

VIII. All French territory should be freed and the invaded portions restored, and the wrong done to France by Prussia in 1871 in the matter of Alsace-Lorraine, which has unsettled the peace of the world for nearly fifty years, should be righted, in order that peace may once more be made secure in the interest of all.

IX. A readjustment of the frontiers of Italy should be effected along clearly recognizable lines of nationality.

X. The people of Austria-Hungary, whose place among the nations we wish to see safeguarded and assured, should be accorded the freest opportunity of autonomous development.

XI. Rumania, Serbia and Montenegro should be evacuated; occupied territories restored; Serbia accorded free and secure access to the sea; and the relations of the several Balkan States to one another determined by friendly counsel along historically established lines of allegiance and nationality; and international guarantees of the political and economic independence and territorial integrity of the several Balkan States should be entered into.

XII. The Turkish portions of the present Ottoman Empire should be assured a secure sovereignty, but the other nationalities which are now under Turkish rule should be assured an undoubted security of life and an absolutely unmolested opportunity of autonomous development, and the Dardanelles should be permanently opened as a free passage to the ships and commerce of all nations under international guarantees.

XIII. An independent Polish State should be erected which should include the territories inhabited by indisputably Polish populations, which should be assured a free and secure access to the sea, and whose political and economic independence and territorial integrity should be guaranteed by international covenant.

XIV. A general association of nations must be formed under specific covenants for the purpose of affording mutual guarantees of political independence and territorial integrity to great and small States alike.

I was as completely lost as a ship in mid-ocean with neither compass nor steering gear; and found myself wandering round and round in circles in the fog. The shelling had become fiercer, and the fog seemed more dense in the smoke of each fresh explosion, which threw up the earth on all sides of me. A 5.9 seemed to land at my very feet, and buried me waist deep. I was not wounded, but felt temporarily stunned, so sat down to get my breath and rest for a few minutes. Hardly knowing what I was doing, I lifted off my Gas Helmet to see things better; and took in a mouthful of Phosgene. I had been fairly calm and collected before, but this made me almost panicky and I felt it was now, indeed, all up with me. However, I pulled myself together...

THE ALLIED COUNTER-OFFENSIVE

On 15 July 1918, the Germans launched their last attack of the war, a push towards Rheims and the River Marne. But the Allies held them in check. Then, three days later, Foch struck back with a vengeance.

On 18 July, the counter-offensive began with a joint operation by the French and Americans. With the aid of about 500 tanks, they pushed the enemy line back 10km. Next came a bigger push in which the British, Australians and Canadians also played a major part. It began at 4.20 am on 8 August, near Amiens in Picardy. Again assisted by tanks, the Allies overwhelmed the German defences. By the evening they had taken over 285 sq km of land. Ludendorff called this the 'black day' of the German army. It no longer had any real prospect of victory.

British Mark V tanks prepare to advance on the Hindenburg Line in September 1918. They carry devices called cribs which were lowered into wide trenches so that the tanks could roll across them.

Colonel George Patton

For most of August, the Allies continued to make gains in Picardy. Then, on 12 September, the Americans attacked the St Mihiel salient, south of Verdun (see map page 50). Half a million US troops took the salient in under 24 hours. Among them was Colonel George Patton, who later played a major role in the Second World War. Soon afterwards, Foch broadened the offensive to include the whole Western Front. On 26 September, the final chapters of the war began to unfold.

The first stage of the new offensive was launched in the Champagne region, around the River Meuse and in the nearby forested district of the Argonne. The Americans under General Pershing led the attack, with the French in support. Rapid early progress slowed as the Germans strengthened their defences and rushed in reinforcements. However, by September the Americans were within reach of the Hindenburg Line (see page 42). Meanwhile, the British under Haig had attacked and broken through the line further north. This was a great achievement.

The Germans had all but lost the war on the battlefield and Ludendorff was cracking under the pressure. In late September,

This painting shows wounded, battle-weary British soldiers who have crossed the Hindenburg Line. In the background, the fighting continues.

he persuaded his government to ask the Allies for an armistice. The request was sent to President Woodrow Wilson on 4 October. However, the peace terms that Wilson offered were harsh and Ludendorff declared his wish to continue the fight instead. Staring military defeat in the face, Germany also had serious problems at home (see pages 54-5).

THE AMERICAN HOME FRONT

Life in the USA altered after it entered the war, just as life on the European home fronts had changed earlier (see pages 28-9). The government-controlled War Industries Board supervised all American factories and told them what to make. The War Labor Board regulated pay and working hours. Many women who already had jobs were re-employed in war industries. The Committee on Public Information was set up to organise censorship and to explain the reasons for the war. It made great use of film as a propaganda medium. One of its productions was *The Kaiser, the Beast of Berlin*.

 ***Im Westen Nichts Neues (All Quiet on the Western Front)* was written by Erich Maria Remarque, a German who served in the First World War. Since its publication in 1929, the novel has become a classic. It tells the story of a group of young German trench soldiers. Here the main character, Paul Bäumer, records his feelings in mid-1918.**

Remarque is referring to the blue of the sky and gold of the sun.

This summer of 1918 is the bloodiest and the hardest. The days are like angels in blue and gold, rising up untouchable above the circle of destruction. Everyone knows that we are losing the war. Nobody talks about it much. We are retreating. We won't be able to attack again after this massive offensive. We have no more men and no more ammunition. But the campaign goes on – the dying continues... Summer 1918, never has life at the front been more bitter and more full of horror than when we are under fire, when the pallid faces are pressed into the mud and the fists are clenched and your whole being is saying, No! No! No, not now! Not now at the very last minute!

IM
WESTEN NICHTS NEUES

VON

ERICH MARIA REMARQUE

*

826.—850. TAUSEND

1929

IM PROPYLÄEN-VERLAG / BERLIN

THE ARMISTICE

By 1918, food shortages in Germany were so severe that many people were forced to search through rubbish for scraps.

By 1918, there was crisis on the German home front. Hunger and disillusion with the war had led to growing discontent with imperial government. People's anger was made worse by the inequalities in German society. A flourishing black market allowed the rich to live well while ordinary people existed on turnips and potatoes.

The Kaiser and his commanders had hoped that success in the March 1918 offensive (see page 50) would bring calm. Its failure brought the opposite. People lost faith in their leaders and the demand for change grew. The Allies' reluctance to enter peace negotiations with the imperial regime added to the pressure for reform.

Finally, on 30 September, Kaiser Wilhelm II signed a decree that brought democratic parliamentary government to Germany. Prince Max von Baden was made the new Chancellor (chief minister). It became his duty, rather than the army's, to negotiate an armistice with the Allies. This was exactly what army commander Erich Ludendorff wanted. The responsibility for Germany's military failure was his. However, he began to blame civilians, claiming that they had not supported the army enough. The decision to ask the Allies for an armistice was also his – but the request was made by the Chancellor. By then rejecting President Wilson's peace terms, Ludendorff was able to insist that the army had always wished to fight on (see page 59).

The Kaiser sacked Ludendorff on 26 October, but as peace terms still could not be agreed, the fighting continued. Then the German authorities ordered the fleet to begin a new campaign at sea. German sailors had been in port since 1916 (see

German officials (standing) arrive to sign the armistice at 5 o'clock on the morning of 11 November 1918. This momentous event took place in a railway carriage in the Forest of Compiègne, northern France.

pages 26-7). During that time, their resentment of domineering officers and of the government had grown. On 29 October, in Kiel and Wilhelmshaven, the sailors mutinied.

Soon the whole country was in uproar and demands for the Kaiser's removal grew. On 8 November, he fled from Berlin and the next day he abdicated. Germany became a republic, led by Friedrich Ebert, and two days later the armistice was signed. At 11a.m. on 11 November, after more than four years of bloody conflict, the ceasefire began.

THE BATTLE OF VITTORIO VENETO

The fighting on the Western Front ended with the 11 November ceasefire. On the Salonika Front (see page 23), the Bulgarians had already signed an armistice on 29 September. In the Middle East, the Turks had signed an armistice on 30 October (see page 49). Italy's defeat at Caporetto (see page 45) was finally reversed on 4 November, when the Austrian army was defeated by a joint Allied force at Vittorio Veneto. It was all over.

Vera Brittain served as a VAD nurse (see page 30) during the war, in London, Malta and France. In 1933, she published an autobiography called *Testament of Youth*, which describes her experiences. Both her brother Edward, and the man she had hoped to marry, Roland, died in the fighting. When the ceasefire began, Vera Brittain was in London. Here she tells of the emotions that she experienced at that time.

When the sound of victorious guns burst over London at 11 a.m. on November 11th 1918, the men and women who looked incredulously into each other's faces did not cry jubilantly: "We've won the War!" They only said: "The War is over."... Late that evening, when supper was over, a group of elated V.A.D.s who were anxious to walk through Westminster and Whitehall to Buckingham Palace prevailed upon me to join them... I detached myself from the others and walked slowly up Whitehall, with my heart sinking in a sudden cold dismay... For the first time I realised, with all that full realisation meant, how completely everything that had hitherto made up my life had vanished with Edward and Roland... The War was over; a new age was beginning; but the dead were dead and would never return.

Desagneaux is referring to the lights of German flares and rockets, not real fireworks.

Henri Desagneaux (see page 13) was still in the trenches when the armistice was signed. This is how he recorded the event.

11 November

Firework display continued all night over in the enemy camp. At 6 a.m., we hear on the radio that the armistice has been signed. The end of hostilities is fixed for 11 a.m. At 11 a.m. it's all over, we are no longer at war. What joy – the champagne flows, the attack won't take place. There's a smile on everyone's lips, no more fighting, we'll be able to move without fearing a bullet, a shell, a rocket, or gas – the war is over!

THE AFTERMATH

The aftermath of the First World War had two aspects: the political and the personal. The main political questions were resolved – at least temporarily – in the Treaty of Versailles, which was drawn up just outside Paris in 1919. Personal matters, from the traumas of shell shock (see box page 57), disfigurement and bereavement to the family readjustments made necessary by the return of soldiers from the war, were addressed in many different ways, with different degrees of success.

The conference intended to thrash out a peace settlement opened in Paris, France, on 18 January 1919. Members of 27 nations attended, but the leading Allied participants were the American and French presidents, Woodrow Wilson and Georges Clemenceau, and the British prime minister, David Lloyd George. Italian prime minister Vittorio Orlando was another important contributor. The Germans sat on the sidelines waiting to hear their fate. Wilson's Fourteen Points (see page 51) formed the basis for the discussion.

Much wrangling followed, especially between the idealistic Wilson and the more practical – and vengeful – Clemenceau.

Five treaties were eventually prepared. The most important was the treaty signed at the Palace of Versailles between the Allies and Germany. The others shared out the land of the Ottoman and Austro-Hungarian empires, and forced Bulgaria to give up some territory.

The Treaty of Versailles was signed on 28 June 1919. Some of the Fourteen Points were included, for example the League of Nations, an organisation designed to preserve peace, was established. However, the treatment of Germany was far more severe than Wilson had envisaged. Germany was declared responsible for the war, and forced to pay massive reparations for the damage caused by the conflict. In addition, the size of its armed forces was strictly limited and its colonies, as well as parts of Germany itself, were taken away (see pages 58-9).

Although this settlement was never accepted by the US Congress, the Germans had no choice but to bow to the treaty's demands. However, the great bitterness and economic upheaval caused by the Versailles agreement directly contributed to the rise of Adolf Hitler and the outbreak of the Second World War only 20 years later, in 1939.

This famous painting by Sir William Orpen shows the signing of the Treaty of Versailles in 1919.

Wilfred Owen served with the Artists' Rifles and Manchester Regiment. His poems were first published in 1920, two years after his death.

PAYING THE PRICE

About nine million men died in the First World War. Many of those who survived had lost limbs or suffered other serious wounds. About 12 per cent of the wounded had facial injuries. It was especially difficult for some of these men to become part of ordinary civilian society once again. Thousands of soldiers also suffered from psychiatric disturbances caused by what they had witnessed. 'Shell shock' took many forms. Some men could not stop shaking, while others could not move. Some laughed hysterically or had delusions.

English war poet Wilfred Owen (above) became shell-shocked in spring 1917. He went to Craiglockhart Hospital in Scotland for treatment, then returned to France, where he was killed a week before the armistice. This is part of his poem 'Disabled'.

He sat in a wheeled chair, waiting for dark,
And shivered in his ghastly suit of grey,
Legless, sewn short at elbow. Through the park
Voices of boys rang saddening like a hymn,
Voices of play and pleasure after day,
Till gathering sleep had mothered them from him.
…
Now, he will spend a few sick years in institutes,
And do what things the rules consider wise,
And take whatever pity they may dole.
To-night he noticed how the women's eyes
Passed from him to the strong men that were
    whole.
How cold and late it is! Why don't they come
And put him into bed? Why don't they come?

This article of the Treaty of Versailles made Germany responsible for the war and demanded reparations.

ARTICLE 231. The Allied and Associated Governments affirm and Germany accepts the responsibility of Germany and her allies for causing all the loss and damage to which the Allied and Associated Governments and their nationals have been subjected as a consequence of the war imposed upon them by the aggression of Germany and her allies…

The Treaty of Versailles, showing the signatures and wax seals of some participants

CONCLUSION

The world that emerged from the cataclysm of the First World War was very different from the one that had entered it over four years earlier. A generation of young men – about 5.4 million from the Allies and about 3.6 million from the Central Powers – had been lost. The civilian population was plunged into mourning. Four empires had fallen and the map of the world been redrawn. The USA had taken on a new role. The effects were so profound and lasting that the conflict became known as the Great War.

The redefining of the world's boundaries, as outlined at Versailles, was a complex business. Alsace-Lorraine was returned to France. A corner of northeast Germany became part of Poland, which had freed itself from Russian rule, as had the Baltic states of Estonia, Latvia and Lithuania. The Rhineland area between France and Germany was occupied by the Allies and the Saarland handed over to League of Nations control for a period of 15 years. Austria, Hungary, Czechoslovakia and Yugoslavia were carved out of the old Austro-Hungarian Empire.

Further afield, France and Britain divided the former German colonies in Africa and the former Turkish territories in the Middle East between themselves. Much of Turkey was given to Greece, but the Turks seized it back and proclaimed an independent republic in 1923.

In this photograph, taken in 1933, Field Marshal Paul von Hindenburg, by then German president, and Adolf Hitler, the new chancellor, sit side by side.

THE NEW EUROPE

Lost by Russia

Lost by Germany

Former Austro-Hungarian Empire

Rhineland area (occupied by Allies)

League of Nations control

0 — 400 miles
0 — 600 km

N

The legacy of all this change was serious instability. Just as before the war, people of one nationality, for example the Germans in Poland, found themselves ruled by people of another. The League of Nations proved unable to prevent growing tension. The Germans began to reassert themselves and, in 1933, Nazi leader Adolf Hitler came to power.

Hitler used the 'stab in the back' theory – Ludendorff's claim that the army had been betrayed by civilians (see page 54) – to justify attacks on anyone who did not agree with his political views. He also assured the Germans, humiliated by the Treaty of Versailles, that their nation would soon be great again. Another world war was in the making.

'For the Fallen', a poem by Laurence Binyon, who served with the Red Cross during the war, is often read on the anniversary of Armistice Day, 11 November. This verse comes from it.

REMEMBERING THE FALLEN

After the war, memorials to the dead were built on the battlefields and in the home towns and villages of those who died. They remain places of pilgrimage. Those who sacrificed their lives are remembered particularly on Armistice Day, 11 November, when many official ceremonies take place at the memorials and elsewhere. The red poppies that covered the battlefields of Flanders in the summer have become a symbol of the dead and in Britain are worn as a tribute.

The opening ceremony, in 1936, of the memorial to the soldiers who fell at Vimy Ridge in France (see page 42)

They shall grow not old, as we that are left grow old:
Age shall not weary them, nor the years condemn.
At the going down of the sun and in the morning
We will remember them.

Many who experienced the horror of trench warfare later portrayed their experiences in words and pictures. Otto Dix was a German artist who fought in the trenches. In words such as these, as well as in his paintings, he conjured up the nightmare of the suffering he experienced.

Lice, rats, barbed wire, fleas, shells, bombs, underground caves, corpses, blood, liquor, mice, cats, artillery, filth, bullets, mortars, fire, steel: that is what war is. It is the work of the devil.

GLOSSARY

Allies The countries that formed the Triple Entente in 1907 (Britain, France and Russia) and later opposed the Central Powers in the First World War. The term also applies to all the other countries that joined their side, including Belgium and Japan (from 1914), Italy (1915) and the USA (1917).

Anzac A member of the Australian and New Zealand Army Corps.

armistice An official agreement between opposing sides to stop fighting in a war.

arms race Rivalry between countries rushing to arm themselves with the best weapons, tanks and other military equipment.

artillery The collective name for cannons and other heavy guns with barrels of a calibre (diameter) of over 20mm.

attrition The gradual process of wearing something or someone down in order to overcome.

Balfour Declaration A letter written by British foreign secretary Arthur Balfour in November 1917. It said that the British government approved of the establishment of a Jewish homeland in Palestine.

Balkans A peninsula in southeastern Europe that in the First World War contained the countries of Albania, Bulgaria, Greece, Montenegro, Romania, Serbia and the European part of the Ottoman Empire.

bayonet A long, thin blade that is attached to a gun so that it extends beyond the end of the barrel. Bayonets are used in hand-to-hand combat.

black market Illegal trade in goods, for example when they are officially restricted by government rationing.

blockade The blocking of access to a particular area in order to prevent people or supplies from reaching it.

Bolshevik A member of the group of Communists that seized power in Russia in 1917. The word 'Bolshevik' means 'majority', because the Bolsheviks formed the greater part of the Russian Social Democratic Party.

British Expeditionary Force (BEF) The first troops that left Britain for mainland Europe in 1914. They were all professional soldiers under the command of Sir John French.

cavalry Troops on horseback.

Central Powers The countries that fought against the Allies in the First World War. They were Germany and Austria-Hungary, both members of the Triple Alliance from 1882, the Ottoman Empire (from 1914) and Bulgaria (1915).

conscientious objector A person who refuses to fight in a war for reasons of conscience – because they believe physical violence to be morally wrong.

conscription Compulsory service in the armed forces.

convoy A group of merchant ships escorted by a group of battle ships for its protection.

corps A group of soldiers, made up of at least two divisions.

counter-battery A battle technique in which artillery from opposing sides fire on each other rather than on attacking troops.

court-martial To try someone in a military court.

division A group of soldiers large enough to act independently. In the First World War, French divisions usually had between 10,000 and 12,000 soldiers. British divisions had about 15,000 soldiers.

Eastern Front The areas of Eastern Europe where opposing armies fought each other during the First World War.

Entente Cordiale The alliance formed between Britain and France in 1904. The name is French for 'friendly understanding'.

field telephone A special type of telephone that can be used in an area where battle is under way.

flame-thrower A weapon that shoots out a stream of burning gas or paraffin.

Flanders An area of Europe that includes parts of Belgium, northern France and the Netherlands.

front line The area of a battlefield reached by the most advanced troops of opposing armies, where they face and fight one another directly.

General Staff The group of officers that help military commanders plan and carry out their operations.

guerrilla A member of a small, often unofficial fighting force. Guerrillas generally specialise in surprise attacks and sabotage.

Hindenburg Line A long line of trenches and other fortifications on the Western Front to which the Germans withdrew in 1917.

home front The areas of countries involved in the war where no fighting took place, but where civilians contributed to the war effort, for example by making weapons or growing food.

howitzer A type of cannon that fired shells high into the air.

incendiary bullet A bullet that is specially designed to start a fire once it hits a target.

infantry Soldiers who fight on foot.

isolationism The policy pursued by some countries of remaining isolated by not participating in international politics.

minesweeper A navy ship that detects mines, then clears or neutralises them so that they cannot explode.

mobilise To assemble troops and prepare for action.

munitions Ammunition, arms and other military equipment.

mustard gas A yellow gas used as a chemical weapon. It caused blisters, burns to the skin and lungs, and sometimes blindness.

No Man's Land The unoccupied area between the front-line trenches of opposing armies.

offensive A major military attack that involves many groups of soldiers acting together to achieve a particular aim.

Ottoman Empire The former empire of the Ottoman Turks, sometimes also known as the Turkish Empire. It lasted from the late 12th century to the end of the First World War. At its height it covered a vast area including parts of Russia, the Middle East, North Africa and southern Europe, as well as Turkey itself.

outflanking A military manoeuvre that involves going around the flank (side) of the enemy, then turning back to surround them.

phosgene A poisonous, colourless gas used as a chemical weapon. It caused victims to choke to death slowly.

propaganda Biased information designed to support a particular cause or damage the reputation of an enemy.

rationing Limiting the availability of food, and sometimes other goods, to small, fixed amounts.

reconnaissance The act of gathering information about enemy activities, for example by flying over their trenches.

reparations Compensation, for example for damage caused in a war. The Germans were ordered to pay reparations after the war in the form of ships, raw materials and other goods, as well as money.

salient A front-line bulge that extends into enemy territory.

Serbs A Slav people who speak Serbo-Croat. Before the First World War, some Serbs lived in the kingdom of Serbia, others in the Austro-Hungarian Empire.

shell Any of various types of explosive missile fired by artillery. Some shells explode in the air, others when they hit a target.

shrapnel Shells containing bullets and pieces of metal that are scattered all around when the shells explode. The word also refers to the bullets and metal pieces themselves.

Slavs A group of peoples from Eastern Europe and Northwest Asia who speak Slavonic languages such as Russian, Polish and Serbo-Croat.

storm trooper A German soldier who did not advance on enemy lines with the main body of troops, but acted independently. Storm troopers used light but deadly weapons such as machine-guns and flame-throwers.

torpedo A cigar-shaped missile that propels itself along under water and is used to attack ships and submarines.

trench fever An infectious disease that causes fever and pain in joints, bones and muscles. It is transmitted by bites from body lice.

trench foot A type of frostbite caused by standing in cold water for a long time. It made feet swell, then go numb. When the swelling went down, the pain became intense.

Triple Alliance The alliance formed by Austria-Hungary, Germany and Italy in 1882.

Triple Entente The alliance formed by Britain, France and Russia in 1907.

U-boat A German submarine. The term is short for *Unterseeboot*, German for 'undersea boat'.

Western Front The areas of France and Belgium in Western Europe where opposing armies faced each other in combat in the First World War.

INDEX